growing by
heart

growing by
heart

scripture memory for women

scharlotte rich

NAVPRESS®

BRINGING TRUTH TO LIFE

OUR GUARANTEE TO YOU

We believe so strongly in the message of our books that we are making this quality guarantee to you. If for any reason you are disappointed with the content of this book, return the title page to us with your name and address and we will refund to you the list price of the book. To help us serve you better, please briefly describe why you were disappointed. Mail your refund request to: NavPress, P.O. Box 35002, Colorado Springs, CO 80935.

The Navigators is an international Christian organization. Our mission is to reach, disciple, and equip people to know Christ and to make Him known through successive generations. We envision multitudes of diverse people in the United States and every other nation who have a passionate love for Christ, live a lifestyle of sharing Christ's love, and multiply spiritual laborers among those without Christ.

NavPress is the publishing ministry of The Navigators. NavPress publications help believers learn biblical truth and apply what they learn to their lives and ministries. Our mission is to stimulate spiritual formation among our readers.

Cover design by David Carlson Design
Cover image: Gary Houlder / CORBIS
Interior art: Brand X Pictures
Creative Team: Terry Behimer, Rachelle Gardner, Darla Hightower, Arvid Wallen, Pat Miller

Some of the anecdotal illustrations in this book are true to life and are included with the permission of the persons involved. All other illustrations are composites of real situations, and any resemblance to people living or dead is coincidental.

Unless otherwise identified, all Scripture quotations in this publication are taken from the HOLY BIBLE: NEW INTERNATIONAL VERSION® (NIV). Copyright © 1973, 1978, 1984 by International Bible Society. Used by permission of Zondervan Publishing House. All rights reserved. Other versions used include: THE MESSAGE (MSG). Copyright © 1993, 1994, 1995, 1996, 2000, 2001, 2002. Used by permission of NavPress Publishing Group; the Holy Bible, New Living Translation (NLT), copyright © 1996. Used by permission of Tyndale House Publishers, Inc., Wheaton, Illinois 60189. All rights reserved; the New King James Version (NKJV). Copyright © 1982 by Thomas Nelson, Inc. Used by permission. All rights reserved; the Contemporary English Version (CEV) © 1995 by American Bible Society. Used by permission.; the Amplified New Testament (AMP), © The Lockman Foundation 1954, 1958; and the King James Version (KJV). Some Scriptures are the author's paraphrase (PP).

Rich, Scharlotte.
  Growing by heart : Scripture memory for women / Scharlotte Rich.
    p. cm.
  Includes bibliographical references.
  ISBN 1-57683-683-5
  1. Christian women--Prayer-books and devotions--English. 2. Christian
women--Religious life. 3. Bible--Memorizing. 4. Gardening--Religious
aspects--Christianity. I. Title.
  BV4844.R54 2004
  242'.643--dc22

                        2004021302

Printed in Canada

1 2 3 4 5 6 7 8 9 10 / 08 07 06 05 04

FOR A FREE CATALOG OF NAVPRESS BOOKS & BIBLE STUDIES,
CALL 1-800-366-7788 (USA) OR 1-416-499-4615 (CANADA)

For all my wonderful women friends,
old and new, who have put up with
the real me and helped me grow.

For my mother and daughters, my high
school friend Kathy L., Jan, Evelyn, my
cool faithful prayer group and my
sporadic but deep Bible study group.

For Jean Fleming, a remarkable author,
who encouraged me to write years ago.

And for Dan,
my college sweetheart of 40 years.

contents

acknowledgments

Thanks to Rachelle Gardner and the great team at NavPress.

Thanks to Evelyn and Kathy for their help and encouragement with the first-read of the manuscript.

A special thank you to a gracious and godly man, Lorne Sanny, of the Navigators, for "How to Spend a Day in Prayer."

They [that delight in God's law] are like trees planted along the riverbank, bearing fruit each season without fail. Their leaves never wither, and in all they do, they prosper.

PSALM 1:3, NLT

I have never known someone leading a spiritually transformed life who had not been deeply saturated in Scripture.

JOHN ORTBERG, *THE LIFE YOU'VE ALWAYS WANTED*

I know of no other single practice in the Christian life more rewarding, practically speaking, than memorizing Scripture.

CHARLES SWINDOLL, *GROWING STRONG IN THE SEASONS OF LIFE*

a soul gardener's guide

Throughout the ages God has spoken to people through the Bible. Christians such as William Tyndale, burned at the stake for translating the Bible into English, died to enable ordinary people like us to read God's Word in our own language. Scripture is a priceless treasure. It is seed for new life and healthy growth. It is spiritual food that makes you strong and comforts you in days of difficulty. It is the undefeatable weapon Christ used against Satan. God's Word will transform your life, revitalize your soul, and bring you into closer fellowship with God.

This book is for women who are His cherished daughters by faith. It is for women who desire to plant God's words deep in their heart.

Growing by Heart is organized so you can memorize one or two verses a week for one year or you can choose your own pace. Read the tips on memorizing and personalize them to fit your learning style. When you finish this devotional, continue to challenge yourself with larger sections of Scripture that speak to your soul. Write down your favorite verses on a pack of spiral bound index cards; set it in your bathroom, kitchen, or office so you can make memorizing Scripture a rewarding lifetime pursuit.

To get the most out of this Scripture-memory devotional, choose a time and a quiet place to which you can retreat several times a week. (For some of us, this means early morning or late at night.) Gather a pen, a prayer journal, and a Bible, and sit down for a refreshing time with God.

On days when time is limited, grab your Scripture-memory card, put it in your purse, and run out the door. The tear-out memory cards in the back of the book give you the choice of memorizing the New International Version (NIV) or the King James Version (KJV) (although I've included other translations in the text). When you finish this book, you will have enriched your life by memorizing fifty to one hundred passages of Scripture, grouped by topic.

After fifty years I still struggle with memorizing Scripture. Intellectually and spiritually, I know that as Scripture becomes part of my heart and soul, I am transformed and become more like Jesus. Yet I let life interfere, gobbling up my time and energy and focus. Still I persevere, however weakly. Some weeks are better than others. Some verses seep into my consciousness like the smell of coffee in the morning. Others are much harder to come by but are well worth the struggle. Either way, God's word blesses my life and it will bless you.

a week of five-minute memory helps

DAY 1.   Write out the verse in your journal. Read the devotional, and then practice the verse aloud several times, putting the reference before and after the verse. (For example: "John 3:16, For God so loved the world. . . . John 3:16"). If possible, ask someone to listen to you say the verse and prompt you. Write down how you can apply it to your life. Put the verse card in a convenient place to review whenever you have a spare moment.

DAY 2.   Write out the verse. Erase key words and practice the verse. Write it once in your own words.

DAY 3.   Copy the key words, then fill in the rest from memory. Put your name in it to personalize it, because God said it to you. Reflect: What does it mean to you personally?

DAY 4.   Review. Make up your own sign language and add physical gestures to accentuate the verse.

DAY 5.   Sing the verse to a tune you know, or make up a tune. Sometimes it's fun to sing verses to music as you are driving. Ask God to use this verse to change your life.

DAY 6.   Try writing out the verse without looking. Review your verse aloud using gestures.

DAY 7.   Draw a simple cartoon picture that reminds you of what the verse means. Each week, review the verses you learned previously. Remember, some verses will be easier to memorize than others. Persevere.

tips for easier memorizing

- Pick the verse and version you are most comfortable with. Keep it fun and personal; this is meant to be a blessing. What works for someone else may not work for you. Reward yourself for success.
- Copy and post the verse several places where you will see it daily: bed table, bathroom mirror, kitchen sink, car (only when stopped in traffic jams!), desktop, computer screen, refrigerator, treadmill, or stationary bike. Get creative! This really helps keep it in your mind.
- Read the words, putting the emphasis on a different word each time, thinking about what the words mean. (Example: *Feed* my sheep. Feed *my* sheep. Feed my *sheep.*)
- Copy the first letter of each key word on the back of the card to jog your memory.
- Ask a family member or a friend to memorize with you.
- Pick a certain time of day to review. Then use unexpected pauses in your day to review.
- Use physical gestures when you practice the verse (Example: for strong, make a muscle; for love, touch your heart; for God, point upward). Sign language is an excellent help.
- Read the verse over several times aloud throughout the day. Think about what the verse means to you personally and how you can apply it to your daily life.
- See it, say it, write it, draw it, sing it! Put it on tape, computer, or PDA so you can review it often. Make those verse cards look used!

- Set reasonable goals for memorizing. Don't give up if you miss a day or a week. Life happens to all of us. Keep the verse cards with you and review them whenever you can.
- Persevere. Picture yourself succeeding.
- Use the blank cards provided in the back of the book for other verses meaningful to you from your personal devotions.
- Find the key word or phrase in the verse. Spend some time meditating on what it means in your life.
- Make two lists: reasons why you want to memorize Scripture and how it benefits your life.
- Ask God to keep verses in your heart and mind, to use them for good in your life and the lives of those around you. Plant. Grow. Bloom.

part 1:

growing in
grace

A life rooted in God combines intimacy and mission, knowledge and action, pulling in and pushing forward, soaking in and giving out, absorbing God and shedding self. It means pressing on while we're letting go, allowing our drivenness to give way to the path of God. It means listening carefully for his leading.

JAN JOHNSON, *LIVING A PURPOSE-FULL LIFE*

[Jesus said,] "Are you tired? Worn out? Burned out on religion? Come to me. Get away with me and you'll recover your life. I'll show you how to take a real rest. Walk with me and work with me — watch how I do it. Learn the unforced rhythms of grace. I won't lay anything heavy or ill-fitting on you. Keep company with me and you'll learn to live freely and lightly."

MATTHEW 11:28-30, MSG

garden party

Joy is mentioned in the Bible hundreds of times. God meant for us to live a life of joy overflowing, shared with family, friends, neighbors, and strangers. Jesus is our example. People were His priority; He spent time one-on-one at small gatherings, large weddings, and dinner parties celebrating life. He even provided the wine. How can we experience the joyous life God intended us to live? By tending our souls.

Picture your soul as a garden. When given proper care and attention, a garden thrives and blooms with gorgeous color, sharing beauty and fragrance with everyone around it. A garden is a great place to have a joyful celebration.

Held many parties in your soul lately? When well-tended, your soul has an overflowing bounty of love that gives joy and sustenance to everyone near you. You reflect love. But we live in a fast, whirling, crazy, sin-filled world with little good in it to feed any soul. So, you need to make soul-tending your personal priority.

"But there's no time in my schedule!" you say. How does a garden look when left untended for a long time? Overgrown with weeds, bugs, snakes, and other critters nesting in piles of dead and twisted growth, choked with vines and prickly nettles. Get the ugly picture? Not exactly a party zone. That's how our souls look when neglected. You can end up useless to yourself and everyone around you. You may fake it for a while, but when storms begin to blow, dry, crumbled little pieces of you fly away in the wind; your life's garden becomes empty and barren, blessing no one.

Begin to nourish yourself with God's Word; even small scraps of Scripture are rich in spiritual vitamins. Jesus said, "Man does not live on bread alone, but on every word that comes from the mouth of God" (Matthew 4:4). Trying to live a godly life without the Bread of Life is like feeding your body a constant diet of junk food. Replace the messages of our empty culture with the life-giving words of Christ. Make memorizing Scripture a lifelong pursuit.

God loves you just as you are, but He wants you to grow even more beautiful. Picture the most beautiful garden since Eden; that's how God wants to nurture your life. Talk about an extreme makeover! You'll grow wiser, stronger, and have lasting inner beauty. As we draw God's words into our hearts, we refresh our souls and experience joy. What a difference that makes in our lives.

JOURNAL THOUGHTS

*How does the world conform you? How does it deplete you? How can memorizing
Scripture limit the world's influence on your life?*

memory verses

1

*Do not conform any longer to the pattern of this world, but be transformed by the
renewing of your mind. Then you will be able to test and approve what God's will
is — his good, pleasing and perfect will.*

ROMANS 12:2

2

*Trust in the LORD with all your heart and lean not on your own understanding; in
all your ways acknowledge him, and he will make your paths straight.*

PROVERBS 3:5-6

The thing about light is that it isn't really yours; it's what you gather and shine back. And it gets more power from reflectiveness; if you sit still and take it in, it fills your cup, and then you can give it off yourself.

ANNE LAMOTT, TRAVELING MERCIES

"I am the light of the world. Whoever follows me will never walk in darkness, but will have the light of life."

JOHN 8:12

sunflowers

Grow anywhere in full sun.

If you have ever seen a field full of sunflowers, you know it is breathtaking. But you will observe a strange phenomenon. All of the blooms in the field face the same direction because they turn their faces to search for the sun. Throughout the day, the flowers move in unison. They twist to follow the sun, as if a giant mechanical hand kept turning them. But it's just part of their God-made nature.

When they are cut and placed in a room, sunflowers reflect the warmth and joy soaked up from the sun that grew them. This cheerful plant is, without a doubt, the easiest plant to grow in a garden, as long as it has sun. Anyone with a birdfeeder knows that sunflowers crop up by themselves everywhere. Some sunflowers grow ten feet high. But gardeners know that all the work they do would be in vain if the sun didn't shine and give life to their efforts.

God put a deep desire in our nature for His Son Jesus Christ. We find life-giving light in Him. The Bible says, "God is light: in him there is no darkness" (1 John 1:5) and "the LORD is my light and my salvation." (Psalm 27:1) Jesus said He is "the light of the world" (John 8:12). We are to live as children of the light, walk in the light, and share it with others. We are to let our light shine in the darkness of the world. To do that, we must keep our faces, hearts, and minds turned toward God. Then, like mirrors, we will reflect the warmth and joy of His light into the dark world around us.

JOURNAL THOUGHTS

Write down some creative ways you could turn your face toward God and soak up some light.

memory verses

3

Let your light shine before men, that they may see your good deeds and praise your Father in heaven.

MATTHEW 5:16

4

Live as children of light (for the fruit of the light consists in all goodness, righteousness and truth) and find out what pleases the Lord.

EPHESIANS 5:8-10

Christ tells us we must lose our life for His sake in order to find it. We discover meaning
and purpose not in the search for self, but in surrender of self, in obedience to Christ.

CHARLES COLSON, *WHO SPEAKS FOR GOD?*

He will lead them to springs of living water.
And God will wipe away every tear from their eyes.

REVELATION 7:17

living water

Sometimes I get so busy with life that I forget to water my garden. If it's winter, I forget to water the houseplants. This happens fairly often. I turn around and see the plants drooping over, dried up, ugly, and lifeless. I can almost hear them gasping. The great thing is that if I remember in time and soak the plants carefully in water, they spring back to life. It's miraculous!

How often in our lives do we do the same thing to our souls? We neglect them, leave them in the dark, with no light or water, until one day we begin holding our throats and gasping and wondering why we can't function very well. Sometimes it takes a life crisis to point this out. Before you get to that point, slow down and spend some quiet time with God. Let Him speak to you with no distractions.

Recently I came across this thought-provoking passage in a book by Michael Yaconelli.

I wonder how many times a day our Father tries to get our attention, tries to quiet us long enough so we can hear His whisper. Many of us grew up believing that every time Jesus is close to us, He wants us to do something: read your Bible more, pray more, share your faith more, go to church more. How would it change your view of Jesus if you believed He doesn't want you to do anything — He just wants to be close to you?[1]

That's a life-changing thought.

Let's ask our Father for living water to rain down so new, green life will burst forth in our lives. Learn to trust Him. Remember that God loves us and we cannot do anything that will make Him love us any more or any less. Soak deeply in streams of living water — His love and grace — and be renewed, as God's people have done over the ages.

JOURNAL THOUGHTS

Grace means there is nothing you can do that will make God love you any more or any less — because He already gave His life for you. How does that affect your to-do list for God? How does it simplify your life? Write one thing you will let go of and trust God to handle.

memory verses

5

Taste and see that the LORD is good; blessed is the [woman] who takes refuge in him.

PSALM 34:8

6

The LORD will guide you always . . . You will be like a well-watered garden, like a spring whose waters never fail.

ISAIAH 58:11

God created humanity for a love relationship with Him. More than anything else, God wants us to love Him with our total being. He is the one who initiates the love relationship. . . . He permitted Jesus to die in order to make it possible. . . . If your love relationship with God is not right, nothing else will be right.

Henry Blackaby and Claude King, *Experiencing God*

So then, just as you received Christ Jesus as Lord, continue to live in him, rooted and built up in him, strengthened in the faith as you were taught, and overflowing with thankfulness.

Colossians 2:6-7

lilies

Countless varieties. Require no special care.

Pastor Dan Baty told a wonderful story to illustrate how God loves us. It went something like this:

> There once was a highly valued wonderful baker who worked for the king. One day the baker had an accident, became paralyzed and unable to work. Every day the king visited the baker and performed an act of service for him. The king kept tending him and the baker came to realize that the king loved him as a person, not just because of his baking ability. The baker heals but is never the same. He is free of the fear of being loved based on his performance. He begins to love and serve

the king in a new way because he knows the king loves him unconditionally.[2]

God loves us regardless of our performance. We are His redeemed, forgiven, dearly loved children. He clothes us in the beauty of His love. On our bad days, He loves us the same as on our best days. He stays beside us and tends us. God comes to all our races and cheers regardless of how we are running that particular day. He doesn't compare us with anyone else. He sees us as more valuable than all the angels, stars, oceans, and glories of all His creation.

What does He expect from us? John 6:28-29 asks the same question and answers it. "What must we do to do the works God requires? . . . The work of God is this: to believe in the one [Jesus] he has sent."

Trust Him. He loves you with a love that isn't measured by your daily performance.

JOURNAL THOUGHTS

Write down one thing you worry about, then give it to God. Every time you begin to worry about it again, give it back to God and practice your verse instead.

memory verses

7

Then Jesus said . . . "Do not worry about your life. . . . Consider how the lilies grow. They do not labor or spin. Yet I tell you, not even Solomon in all his splendor was dressed like one of these."

LUKE 12:22,27

8

Being confident of this, that he who began a good work in you will carry it on to completion until the day of Christ Jesus.

PHILIPPIANS 1:6

With the goodness of God to desire our highest welfare, the wisdom of God to plan it,
what do we lack? Surely we are the most favored of all creatures.

A. W. TOZER, *THE KNOWLEDGE OF THE HOLY*

Live a lover's life . . . a life Jesus will be proud of: [a life] bountiful in fruits from the soul.

PHILIPPIANS 1:10-11, MSG

sowing seeds

Jesus tells several stories about farmers sowing seeds. Some seed stayed on hard ground and was trampled or eaten by birds, some seed was scattered on rocks and dried up from lack of water, some was choked by weeds and thorns, but some grew in good soil and produced a bountiful harvest.

Jesus explained that the seed was God's Word in the world and Jesus is the Sower. Some people merely hear and don't believe. Some feel a momentary emotional response but decide not to follow Christ. Others let the world and love of money and things strangle their faith. The seed in good soil refers to people who hear and understand the gospel, repent, thank God, and seek to know Him. They begin to grow and live fruitful lives obeying God.

You've heard the good news that God died and rose again to save your soul and the souls of everyone around you. What you do with that truth determines the direction your life and the lives of people you touch. Persevere and get to know Him intimately. Read the Bible; it's all about you and Him. Talk to Him in prayer and seek His will. It will make the growing by heart

difference between a dry, weed-choked life and one that is fruitful in ways you cannot begin to imagine.

32

JOURNAL THOUGHTS

Read Luke 8 and Matthew 13:3-43. Write in your journal, "I don't need to do anything to earn the love of God. That's grace." Remember that today.

memory verses

9

I am the way and the truth and the life. No one comes to the Father except through me.

JOHN 14:6

10

But because of his great love for us, God, who is rich in mercy, made us alive with Christ even when we were dead in transgressions — it is by grace you have been saved.

EPHESIANS 2:4-5

part 2:

growing in
faith

We only get one life to build for the glory of God. . . . You can hold back and hesitate. You can live in fear and respond half-heartedly. There is nothing to hoard, because God replenishes so freely. . . . He's wild about you. Do whatever it takes. Spend it all, my friend. Spend it all.

ANGELA THOMAS, *A BEAUTIFUL OFFERING*

And without faith it is impossible to please God, because anyone who comes to him must believe that he exists and that he rewards those who earnestly seek him.

HEBREWS 11:6

the master gardener

There are many cheap imitations and poor copies of the real thing. Gardeners may try to save money by buying plants, seeds, and bulbs at discount stores or from colorful magazine ads that scream with marketing hype: "Buy 300 bulbs for only $5.99!" "Plant trees that will grow fifteen feet the first year!" Disappointment sets in when the results don't live up to the promises. The same hype is found in religion. False teachers and fakers are still around. Don't be fooled. There is one true God, maker of heaven and earth. Your Creator is the real thing and He doesn't disappoint.

God's presence in our lives is real. The Bible in the Old Testament describes a God who cares for His children tenderly but who jealously guards them. Time after time, His people got into trouble because they dallied with following after other things and man-made gods. Jesus, representing His Father God, said He was the *only* way into heaven and eternal life.

My first grandchild was born a skeptic. It has taken me many hours of time to win her trust. She had to learn from experience. She had to encounter and test my love for her over and over before she could know that she could give her heart to me. Now, even in a strange environment like a hotel pool, she will unthinkingly take my hand and jump off the side of the pool into deep water, trusting me to catch her and keep her safe. She giggles and laughs as she jumps into the uncertain depths of the pool, because she knows, loves, and trusts me.

God is willing to woo us in the same way. He loves you fiercely, but He will not push you beyond where you are capable of trusting. God is trustworthy; He is a strong and safe refuge. Make getting to know Jesus your first priority. Read and study the Bible, talk often with God in prayer. Meet with other Christians regularly. Ask older Christians to share how God has proved faithful in their lives. Experience His love and faithfulness by stepping out in faith. Jump into deep water with confidence. Don't just take someone else's word for it. Go to the source. He gives an eternal lifetime guarantee.

JOURNAL THOUGHTS

Write down one thing you are trusting God for this week. Whenever you see money, read the inscription: "In God we trust." It's a great reminder in the middle of a busy day.

memory verses

11

Peace I leave with you; my peace I give you. I do not give to you as the world gives. Do not let your hearts be troubled and do not be afraid.

JOHN 14:27

12

The LORD is my rock, my fortress and my deliverer . . . He is my stronghold, my refuge and my savior.

2 SAMUEL 22:2–3

The most influential factor in the Christian life is our concept of God. I look at God in two ways. One is that His love is unconditional — there were no preconditions for salvation, and there are no preconditions for maintaining salvation. The second is that His forgiveness and restoration are absolute and complete. The Christian life is not a result of our performance; it's a result of grace. We perform out of gratitude for who we are.

JIM DOWNING, THE NAVIGATORS[1]

Jesus did many other miraculous signs in the presence of his disciples, which are not recorded in this book. But these are written that you may believe that Jesus is the Christ, the Son of God, and that by believing you may have life in His name.

JOHN 20:30-31

daisies

Bloom freely. Hardy, adaptable, especially treasured.

Ever play that game with a daisy, picking its petals off one by one? You know, the "He loves me, he loves me not" thing? A lot of times I subconsciously do that with God. If my life is going well, I think, "He loves me." If things begin to go downhill fast, I think, "Whoops! He loves me not." If I have done something good for others, I think, "He loves me." If I harbor sin, I think, "He *really* loves me not." I'm like a Girl Scout earning badges. Sometimes even when all is going well with my actions and my life, my hormones and emotions get me down, and I think, *I am unlovable. He* must *love me not.*

Many Christians play the daisy game, and play it often. We play it all our lives. It comes from a variety of sources but the result is the same. We don't feel lovable. We think we need to earn God's love. We live on an emotional, irrational roller coaster of unworthiness because we're human. Humans don't love unconditionally. Humans don't immediately forgive and cover others with grace. We're too . . . human.

It's hard for humans to understand God and to take Him at His word. That's part of why He had to send His Son to earth in human form; He wanted our finite human minds to understand an infinite, loving God. He wanted us to understand the message that God, who made us and the entire universe, from stars to slugs, sees us as His dearly loved children.

Imagine! He loves me! He loves you! Let's live bravely like secure and cherished children. Let's believe Him and stop playing the stupid daisy game. Let's weave daisy chain crowns for our heads and dance in the world with joy instead. For we have a wonderful, trustworthy God in whom we place our faith.

JOURNAL THOUGHTS

God loves you just as you are. Write the name of someone who needs to know this and pray for them.

memory verses

13

For God so loved the world that he gave his one and only Son, that whoever believes in him shall not perish but have eternal life. For God did not send his Son into the world to condemn the world, but to save the world through him.

JOHN 3:16-17

14

But God demonstrates his own love for us in this: While we were still sinners, Christ died for us.

ROMANS 5:8

With his own pierced hands, Jesus created a pasture for the soul. He tore out the thorny underbrush of condemnation. He pried loose the huge boulders of sin. In their place he planted seeds of grace and dug ponds of mercy. And he invites us to rest there.

MAX LUCADO, TRAVELING LIGHT

The LORD himself goes before you and will be with you; he will never leave you nor forsake you. Do not be afraid; do not be discouraged.

DEUTERONOMY 31:8

shepherd's hedge

Herding sheep was a major occupation in the time and place when Jesus walked and taught on earth. At night the shepherd would pile up brush, brambles, sticks, or stones, whatever materials were available, to make a hedge of protection around the sheep. Each hedge had a threefold job: to keep predators out, to give shelter from the weather, and to keep sheep from wandering away. Sheep are dumb. They were prone to wandering on their own, getting lost, hurt, eating poisonous plants, or being eaten by predators.

If necessary, the shepherd would build a new hedge every night, as the sheep kept moving to forage for food. Everything the sheep needed was provided by the shepherd: food, water, companionship, leadership, and protection. He would even fight off wild animals. If one sheep was lost, he would make sure the others were safe, then go off and find the missing one. The sheep lacked nothing. At night, the shepherd would often sing or play music to calm the sheep so they could hear his voice.

God is our shepherd. He hedges us in. He promises that we will not lack anything essential. He pledges to love us and extend mercy to us all the days of our lives. He keeps hedges of protection around us and walks close to us so we don't need to fear evil. He shepherds us on the right path and sings to us on dark nights. He will search for us when we are lost and restore our souls. If we follow Him and listen to His voice, we shall lack nothing. The lives of sheep are brief, and they may live in rocky, dangerous land, but the Shepherd is always with them. The Lord is my Shepherd. I shall lack nothing.

JOURNAL THOUGHTS

Begin a written list of prayer requests and their answers. It will strengthen your faith in the future to look back at how God was faithful. How does "asking" both demonstrate your faith and help your faith grow?

memory verses

15

The LORD is my shepherd, I shall not be in want. He makes me lie down in green pastures, he leads me beside quiet waters, he restores my soul. He guides me in paths of righteousness for his name's sake. Even though I walk through the valley of the shadow of death, I will fear no evil, for you are with me; your rod and your staff, they comfort me. You prepare a table before me in the presence of my enemies. You anoint my head with oil; my cup overflows. Surely goodness and love will follow me all the days of my life, and I will dwell in the house of the LORD forever.

PSALM 23, THE SHEPHERD'S SONG

16

[Christ said,] "I am the good shepherd. The good shepherd lays down his life for the sheep."

JOHN 10:11

How then to have our faith increased? . . . Not a striving to have faith . . . but a looking off to the Faithful One seems all we need; a resting in the Loved One entirely, for time and for eternity.

HUDSON TAYLOR, *HUDSON TAYLOR'S SPIRITUAL SECRET*

The God who made the world and everything in it is the Lord of heaven and earth . . . he himself gives all men life and breath and everything else.

ACTS 17:24-25

dusk

One of the most pleasant things to do around a garden is to simply sit and enjoy it. Dusk is a lovely time to do this, when life is still, balanced between daylight and darkness. Sit quietly some night and watch as the stars begin to come out one by one until all of a sudden the sky is full of jewels.

As your eyes get used to the dark, more and more stars appear. They have always been there; you just couldn't see them. Psalm 147 says God decides how many stars there are and takes the time to name each one. He looks at the earth and sends rain for green pastures; He keeps the earth spinning, the sun shining.

But while running the entire universe, God's real joy is in people who reverence Him. We often find irritation, not joy, in people; but the Bible says that God finds joy in us. Not in playing marbles with the stars or staging whale races or erupting volcanoes, but in hanging out with — people!

God loves being with us. What a mind-blowing thought!

Take some time this week to read Psalms 146 and 147. Be encouraged, knowing that the same God who created the universe knows your name, cares for you, finds joy in spending time with you, wants to wipe your tears, heal your wounds, and give you love, joy, and peace. Peace, like you find just sitting in the garden at dusk, not alone but with an awesome Father who understands you. A Father who loves you more than all the stars in the universe. A Father you can trust with your life, worthy of your faith because He is good, eternally trustworthy.

JOURNAL THOUGHTS

What are some expectations implied in a loving father-child relationship? Define your present relationship with God. Ask God to strengthen your faith in Him.

memory verses

17

Be still, and know that I am God; I will be exalted among the nations, I will be exalted in the earth.

PSALM 46:10

18

He calls his own sheep by name and leads them out. . . . My sheep listen to my voice; I know them, and they follow me. I give them eternal life, and they shall never perish; no one can snatch them out of my hand.

JOHN 10:3,27-28

It is the very time for faith to work, when sight ceases. The greater the difficulties, the easier for faith.

GEORGE MUELLER, GEORGE MUELLER OF BRISTOL

Everyone who hears these words of mine and puts them into practice is like a wise man who built his house on the rock. The rain came down, the streams rose, and the winds blew and beat against that house; yet it did not fall, because it had its foundation on the rock.

MATTHEW 7:24-25

love in a mist

Full sun or partial shade. Self-sower.

Self-sowers. I love these plants. You put them in the ground and they grow. Then they plant more of themselves, spreading over the bare earth, covering it with beauty. They send out runners or give off seeds that go into the ground and multiply their beauty in the seasons to come.

I re-read the autobiography of George Mueller recently. He was a self-sower. He took a need that God put on his heart and he began working on it. An ordinary young man in the 1800s in England, Mueller believed God wanted him to start a small orphanage. He never asked people for money for the orphanage but prayed directly to God for their needs. Eventually more than 100,000 children were fed, clothed, housed, and educated. The faith of this one man was also responsible for eighty-two missionaries sent out and thousands of Bibles and tracts given away. All because one person took God at His word and acted on it.

God can multiply our smallest efforts and spread blessings to many. Jesus fed thousands with one small lunch offered in service. He compared the kingdom of God to a tiny mustard seed. The mustard seed is the smallest garden seed, but when planted it grows so large that birds roost in its shade. Don't believe Satan when he whispers in your ear that you are insignificant, that you cannot make a difference for good in this world. History is filled with men and women who said "yes" to God and changed the course of the world.

Is there something good God keeps nudging you about? Jump in! Get started. Be a self-sower. If God wants you to do something, go ahead by faith. He has promised to supply all that you need. He will multiply your efforts. As a Texas pastor once said, instead of "If God is willing, and the creek don't rise," say "If God is willing, the creek don't matter!" God is omnipotent, all-powerful. Is anything too hard for him?

JOURNAL THOUGHTS

As a woman loved by God, what are you trusting Him for? Place something or someone entirely in God's hands, and then step back and watch Him work.

memory verses

19

Ask and it will be given to you; seek and you will find; knock and the door will be opened to you. For everyone who asks receives; he who seeks finds; and to him who knocks, the door will be opened.

MATTHEW 7:7-8

20

And God is able to make all grace abound to you, so that in all things at all times, having all that you need, you will abound in every good work.

2 CORINTHIANS 9:8

The Pharisees knew the Scripture inside and out but missed the heart of God. The Bible is not primarily a manual for living, a sourcebook of sayings, a treasure of spiritual nuggets, or even a roadmap to heaven. It is a book that reveals to us who God is and how we can enter into a relationship with him through Jesus Christ.

JOHN FISCHER[2]

This is what the LORD says to you: "Do not be afraid or discouraged because of this vast army. For the battle is not yours, but God's."

2 CHRONICLES 20:15

oak trees and deep roots

Oak trees and people can grow stronger roots with stress. When I think of oak trees, I think of several of my friends who are strong women. One, in particular, doesn't look much like an oak; she is petite, joyful, and energetic. Her crinkly smile starts in her eyes and spreads to everyone around her. If you didn't know her, you would think her life was carefree. Yet she always has a huge amount of stressful things going on in her life: job, family concerns, health problems, and many hurting people she ministers to. She stays strong and joyful because she meets with Jesus daily; she knows that He loves her and listens to her prayers.

Look beyond the surface and most women are carrying an enormous load. Along with family, job, and personal sorrows, women are caretakers. They minister to the brokenhearted, the sick, the young, the handicapped, the homeless, and the elderly. They volunteer and they are drafted. They also get involved in national concerns, moral issues, community needs, and in contacting and praying for our nation's leaders. Even though we try to structure our time and priorities, it's still easy to get stressed out. The only alternative is to trust God with our daily lives.

Give the needs of each day to God and trust Him with it. Start and end your days with prayer, asking the Lord to order your day according to His will. Then plunge ahead fearlessly, secure in your faith that He will do it. He's sure to make an adventure of an ordinary day.

We will always have stress in our lives. Ask God to use the difficult things in your life to grow your roots stronger into the love of Christ. Like an oak.

JOURNAL THOUGHTS

Write down your top two priorities for this week. Ask God for His top two priorities for your week. How well do they match?

memory verses

21

And my God will meet all your needs according to his glorious riches in Christ Jesus.
PHILIPPIANS 4:19

22

Do not fear, for I am with you; do not be dismayed, for I am your God. I will strengthen you and help you; I will uphold you with my righteous right hand.
ISAIAH 41:10

Much greater ability and knowledge come from storms and unfamiliar terrain than from fair weather and a well-trodden path, providing one persists and prevails.

DEE HOCK, CEO, VISA INTERNATIONAL

In God I trust; I will not be afraid.

PSALM 56:4

riding out storms

A gnarled old tree came crashing down in the garden last night. Broken limbs and twigs were scattered all over the lawn. Fierce autumn storms brought terrific winds that pulled and dragged down the giant. It had been drastically weakened at its roots by several years of drought. It was like mourning the loss of an old friend; it had given its shade in summer, twigs for toddlers playing imaginary games under its leaves, and strong limbs for swings and climbing. Even now it would provide firewood to keep the family warm throughout the cold winter.

People need to develop deep roots of faith and drink from Christ's living water supply so they will be ready to face drought and storms. Some people appear to go through life without much stress. But the reality is that everyone will battle many fierce storms of one type or another, whether their struggle is evident to others or not. Jesus did not protect His disciples from experiencing storms. But He did warn them of hard times to come, helped them prepare, and then rode through the wind of the storms with them. When they became overwhelmed, He even calmed the storm.

After a big storm, there is always a lot of breakage to clean up. Take time in your life, after a difficult episode, to pick up all the pieces. Let God hold you and comfort you in His mighty arms. Don't rush to smile and pretend that the storm never happened. Be real about your feelings. Take time to heal. Drink deeply of Christ's living water and the solace of friends. Ask God to gently teach you any lessons to be learned.

When Jesus finally left earth, He did not leave us alone and helpless — He gave us mighty weapons to use against hard times. He left the permanent shelter of His love and grace. He gave His Spirit to ride through the storms with us. He left an emergency phone line always open direct to God, called prayer. He gave us the love of other Christians. And He left the shining sword of the Spirit, the Word of God, as the ultimate weapon of defense.

JOURNAL THOUGHTS

Please read Ephesians 6:10-20. List some of God's strengths as a protector.

memory verses

23

Be strong in the Lord and in his mighty power. Put on the full armor of God so that you can take your stand against the devil's schemes.

EPHESIANS 6:10-11

24

The one who is in you is greater than the one who is in the world.

1 JOHN 4:4

part 3:

growing in contentment

*My garden is an honest place. Every tree and every vine are incapable of concealment,
and tell after two or three months exactly what sort of treatment they have had.
The sower may mistake and sow his peas crookedly; the peas make no
mistake but come and show his line.*

RALPH WALDO EMERSON, *JOURNALS OF RALPH WALDO EMERSON*

Just think: a life conceived by God himself!

1 PETER 1:23, MSG

reflecting the sower

A garden is a very reliable thing: If you plant peas, peas will come up. You
never have to wonder when you plant purple petunias if a crop of onions
will come up instead. Whether you sow seeds spread closely or thinly,
crooked or straight as a ruler, your plants will grow as you planted them.
A garden reflects the sower.

Do you ever wonder if God made a mistake with you? Ever wonder
if He put you in the wrong place or whether He made some part of you
incorrectly? Think you don't measure up to some of the other plants in
His garden? That maybe you are really (gasp) a *weed* but no one has found
out yet? That you are a skunk cabbage in a rose garden?

If so, the Bible says you are wrong, wrong, wrong. God formed you in
a wonderful way; He planned a purpose for your life that no one else can
fill. You are amazingly unique and special. God wants you to be yourself
and to use your gifts that He gave you in a positive way that reflects glory

back to your Creator. There is a special niche in His garden that only you can fill with the beauty, color, and shape that He gave you. God is the master gardener; He does *not* make mistakes.

JOURNAL THOUGHTS

Make a short list of gifts God has given you in abilities and interests. Plan to use one of your special, unique gifts to encourage someone else.

memory verses

25

Know therefore that the LORD your God is God; he is the faithful God, keeping his covenant of love to a thousand generations of those who love him and keep his commands.

DEUTERONOMY 7:9

26

I praise you because I am fearfully and wonderfully made; your works are wonderful, I know that full well.

PSALM 139:14

In the depth of winter, I finally learned that within me there lay an invincible summer.
ALBERT CAMUS

There is a time for everything, and a season for every activity under heaven . . . a time to weep and a time to laugh, a time to mourn and a time to dance.
ECCLESIASTES 3:1-4

seasons

Life is not fair. Yesterday we had an early, hard frost and all the flowers crumpled into sodden masses. Today the temperature is in the high seventies; the sun is cheerily beaming down on a ruined garden that cannot bloom again until spring. The weather forecast is for sunny days all week. Why did the premature frost have to come and ruin everything we worked on all summer? Why couldn't there have been more lovely days to sit and enjoy the garden's riot of color?

Life is *not* fair, and things that are far more terrible occur in our lives. People die, homes burn down, soldiers don't return from war. Health fails, marriages break apart, savings disappear. Hard times eventually come to everyone.

But then there are seasons of joy, light, and gladness. Love blooms, babies are born, jobs go well, families come together for celebrations. Puppies wag tails; the sun shines; oceans, mountains, and lakes show us a faint glimpse of the beauty and creativity of their Maker; and our hearts feel at peace.

How do we balance the seasons of life? How do we make sense of good and evil, joy and gladness juxtaposed so closely in our lives? Especially when the hard times seem to come in clusters. There is no easy answer, but understanding that God is absolutely good and trustworthy is the first key. Learning to live one day at a time, trusting God for that day, is the second.

In response to his hard life, sold into slavery by his brothers, Joseph answered that it was meant to be an evil experience but God turned it around and used it for good. If we stay close to Him, God uses everything, good and bad, in our lives to help us grow more like Jesus. If our view of God allows us to see Him as a loving father who desires the best for us, then we must trust Him with our daily lives.

Good and bad will happen to us all. As our trust grows over the years, we can let go of all the "stuff" in our lives that we worry about. We can look for and enjoy the good things of each day. We can trust God to walk with us through good times and times of frost. We learn, as Paul did over time and through many trials, to say, "I have learned the secret of being content in any situation. . . . I can do everything through Him who gives me strength" (Philippians 4:12-13).

JOURNAL THOUGHTS

Please read Ecclesiastes 3:1-15. Write a prayer about something in your life that has been very difficult. Ask God to use it for good.

memory verses

27

And we know that in all things God works for the good of those who love him, who have been called according to his purpose.

ROMANS 8:28

28

I have learned the secret of being content in any and every situation. . . . I can do everything through him who gives me strength.

PHILIPPIANS 4:12-13

One of the ways our faith expresses itself is by our ability to be still,
to be present, and not to panic or lose perspective. God still does
his best work in the most difficult of circumstances.

TIM HANSEL, *YOU GOTTA KEEP DANCIN'*

Pile your troubles on GOD's shoulders — he'll carry your load, he'll help you out.

PSALM 55:22, MSG

garden bench time

Jesus gave us the best examples of dealing with stress. He always found time to be alone with God, even in the midst of His demanding ministry. Gardens and the outdoors gave Jesus joy and a quiet place to think and pray. He rowed across lakes; He walked in the wilderness. He followed God's timetable even when pressed to rush to the side of a dying friend. When He was preparing to give His life for us on the cross, He made time to be still in a garden and pray.

Take time to sit and examine your life regularly. Look for things that add unnecessary stress and cut them out of your life. I used to listen to talk radio on my way to work. I finally turned it off because it was negative poison pouring into my brain. Most television programming is full of immoral junk and commercials telling me that I never have enough stuff. What things in your life add stress? How can you eliminate or change them? What positive things can you put in their place?

We need to plan for daily quiet times with God. But plan at least once a year (more often if possible) to get a full day or a weekend just to be quiet somewhere away from your normal responsibilities. Sit and listen to God; talk with Him. If you are married, you can also do this as a couple. Write it in your schedule like your yearly physical or dentist visit. It's even more essential to your well-being. Take a pen, paper or journal, and your Bible. Maybe you can bring along a favorite Christian book.

In the appendix (page 193) are tips from The Navigators' pamphlet called *How to Spend a Day in Prayer,* which can help you get started with extended quiet times. Try it. A little "garden bench" time will change your life.

JOURNAL THOUGHTS

List the first things that come into your head when you think about stress in your life. Hand these stresses over to God. Ask Him to give you creative ideas on dealing with them in a proactive way. Write down some positive plans.

memory verses

29

Be very careful, then, how you live — not as unwise but as wise, making the most of every opportunity, because the days are evil. Therefore do not be foolish, but understand what the Lord's will is.

EPHESIANS 5:15-17

30

Do not be anxious about anything, but in everything, by prayer and petition, with thanksgiving, present your requests to God. And the peace of God, which transcends all understanding, will guard your hearts and your minds in Christ Jesus.

PHILIPPIANS 4:6-7

Let Him put you on his wheel and whirl you as he likes, and as sure as God is God and you are you, you will turn out exactly in accordance with [His] vision. Don't lose heart in the process.

OSWALD CHAMBERS, *MY UTMOST FOR HIS HIGHEST DEVOTIONAL*

We are the clay, you are the potter; we are all the work of your hand.

ISAIAH 64:8

clay pots

In New Mexico, there are lots of wonderful roadside stands full of quirky and interesting things. There's always a variety of fruits and vegetables in season, including long ristras of cascading red peppers. Colorful blankets, wide straw hats, bright serapes, and sombreros. And pottery. Lots and lots of pottery. I purchased a red clay pitcher made in the shape of an amused owl. It looks ordinary from the back but there is this astonishing face peering out at you from the front. You can find pottery donkeys and flowers and every kind of shape and form you can think of. There are pots with special holes to grow strawberries and other cascading plants. There are long pots, small pots, round pots, square pots. There are shiny pots and sculptures in a wild variety of shapes and forms. The creativity is only limited to the mind and skill of the potter.

God compares us to clay in His hands. He shapes us with different pressures and molds us as He sees fit. He has a purpose; a use for each one of us, and it is not the same one as the person next to us. We are unique.

But inwardly we are all to be conformed to the image of Christ. So outwardly we have different uses, but inwardly we have the same spirit, the same love, the same beauty of soul, the same possibilities, because the Potter made us that way.

God creates us all for distinct times and purposes. Therefore, I never have to look at my friend or neighbor and grumble that I am not like her. I can rest in the fact that God made me the way I am and put me where I am for a reason. When you look around you, notice how many different uses and shapes God has for people. Thank Him for His unlimited artistic creativity.

JOURNAL THOUGHTS

Write a note to God and thank Him for the way He made you. Ask Him to do some-thing unique and beautiful with your life.

memory verses

31

Do nothing out of selfish ambition or vain conceit, but in humility consider others better than yourselves . . . look not only to your own interests, but also to the interests of others. Your attitude should be the same as that of Christ Jesus.

PHILIPPIANS 2:3-5

32

For we are God's workmanship, created in Christ Jesus to do good works, which God prepared in advance for us to do.

EPHESIANS 2:10

Dark days will not last forever. The light will always return to chase away the darkness, the sun will always come out again after the rain, and the human spirit will always rise above failure. Fear will assault us, but we will not be afraid, "for Thou art with me."

HAROLD S. KUSHNER, *THE LORD IS MY SHEPHERD*

So I will restore to you the years that the swarming locust has eaten.

JOEL 2:25, NKJV

locusts

During the dust bowl years in America, farmers in the West were struggling to eke out an existence on their family farms. But not only did they have to deal with the dust and wind that carried away the good topsoil. If they got anything to grow, sometimes hordes of hungry locusts (grasshoppers) would appear from nowhere. Thousands of these voracious bugs would swarm across the fields, devouring everything in sight. Looking at my garden after two or three of these critters have nibbled plants down to stubs, I cannot imagine the sorrow and devastation experienced by families who relied on what they grew to survive. Many families gave up, packed their meager belongings, and simply left their homesteads and fields to the disaster. It took them years to get back to where they were before the locusts came. Many never made it, becoming homeless or committing suicide. In the Bible, God used locusts to destroy the food of the enemies of Israel. They have become a symbol of devastation and loss.

When I was a young woman, I remember talking with an older and wiser friend about feeling guilty because my life was going so well at the time, compared to many others in the world. "Just enjoy it," she said. "We will all have our hard times and trials. Enjoy where you are right now. Be thankful to God for everything and don't feel guilty." And of course, she was right.

We'll all experience times of "locusts." We may never understand why they come. Sometimes they may be sent by God to get our attention back on Him. Or He may want us to grow more in a certain area of Christian character. Sometimes they are the result of the sin of others. Sometimes they seem to come without rhyme or reason, just from living in a fallen world. But God is still in control. He still loves us. He still gives us good gifts, even in the midst of pain, difficulty, and sorrow. We may have to look harder for them but they are there. We need to seek Him for comfort and refuge. Trust Him to care for you even when the locusts come.

Journal Thoughts

Whether you are in a time of joy or a time of sorrow in your life, read Lamentations 3:25-26. Write down your response.

memory verses

33

God is our refuge and strength, an ever-present help in trouble. Therefore we will not fear, though the earth give way and the mountains fall into the heart of the sea. . . . The LORD Almighty is with us; the God of Jacob is our fortress.

PSALM 46:1-2,7

34

Consider it pure joy, my [sisters], whenever you face trials of many kinds, because you know that the testing of your faith develops perseverance. Perseverance must finish its work so that you may be mature and complete, not lacking anything.

JAMES 1:2-4

Envy is the art of counting someone else's blessings instead of your own.

But godliness with contentment is great gain.

1 TIMOTHY 6:6

greener grass

I looked at my garden and was very happy with it, until I looked over the fence at my neighbor's garden. All of a sudden, my garden was lacking. The squash looked puny. The colors weren't as cool. I could see the weeds in the corner. I didn't have a flowering vine. Her grass looked . . . greener. I became discontented.

Meeting a friend for dinner, I was happy. Even my hair was having a good day. Then my tall, beautiful friend appeared. She had gotten her makeup done, lost weight, and wore a great new outfit. I love my friend and was happy for her, but I felt discontentment. Why couldn't I have spent the day getting pampered, or be three inches taller? I have everything I need and more, yet when I look at magazines or television or the salaries of superstars, I become discontented. Whenever I take my eyes off God and compare myself with others, I focus on what I don't have, what I think I need.

Even in biblical times, God's people were dissatisfied. He did marvelous things for them, they would be thankful for a time, but then they would forget and begin to grumble. He would reprimand them, they would be sorry, He would forgive them, and then they would forget and start to grumble all over again! Just read Exodus. Satan loves to stir up discontentment because, when we complain, we are stating that God isn't good enough to us. As if giving us the life of His only Son wasn't enough by itself.

God says we are to make music in our hearts as we give thanks. If we begin and end our days by counting our blessings and sharing them, there won't be any time to dwell on what we don't have or look at what our neighbor has. Being thankful prevents greediness, envy, and lots of other sins. You begin to notice how green your own grass (or is that grace?) really is.

Journal Thoughts

Instead of counting someone else's blessings, count your own. Make a list of things you are thankful for, beginning with the love of Christ. Start a prayer with "I am blessed because . . ." This is a great, calming activity when you are feeling stressed at night.

memory verses

35

Keep your lives free from the love of money and be content with what you have, because God has said, "Never will I leave you; never will I forsake you."

HEBREWS 13:5

36

A generous [woman] will prosper; [she] who refreshes others will [herself] be refreshed.

PROVERBS 11:25

part 4:

growing in purity

An old Arab proverb says, "What is the greatest crime in the desert?
Finding water and keeping silent."

ARAB WORLD MINISTRIES

Whoever drinks the water I give [her] will never thirst. Indeed, the water I give [her]
will become in [her] a spring of water welling up to eternal life.

JOHN 4:14

the wellspring

When I was a child, I remember visiting an elderly great-aunt in the beautiful mountains of Virginia. In order to enter her home, a hanging bridge had to be crossed, a fairly rickety thing of wood and wire that would sway as you crossed over the rushing stream full of rocks below it. It was very different from anything I had ever experienced. All we had at home was a short concrete sidewalk. For a city girl, there were even more wonderful things to discover. Aside from several large and wooly dogs, assorted cats, a vegetable garden, berry bushes, and flowers growing everywhere, there was the wellspring.

Even though she had electricity, my aunt still valued some old ways. Several yards away from the house, under a beautiful old tree, there was a springhouse. This was a small stone and wooden structure that covered the wellspring. The wellspring was the spot where icy cold water bubbled up freely from the earth. The mountain spring water was crisp and cool, even on a hot, humid August day in the South. Milk, cream, watermelon, apples, and other perishables were kept in there so they wouldn't spoil.

The spring supplied water for the stream and for the garden; it gave water for drinking and washing at the house. A small, green salamander lived near there to keep the bugs away. Surely, the reason the house was originally built in that location was the availability of fresh water from the spring. The source was hidden; it must have come from a plentiful underground river. It refreshed everyone who lived or visited there. It was a life-giving thing.

The Bible says to guard your heart for it is the wellspring of life. Our heart is the core of our being, fed by the deep, living water of Christ. Once He fills it, it is full for eternity. We need to guard it and keep it clean from pollutants. Sin will muddy its waters. God's grace will cleanse it.

What are some simple ways to guard your heart? First, prevent the wrong things from getting into it. The world constantly pushes unworthy things in front of us. Guard what you see, listen to, and think about. Confess sin and repent so God's grace can keep your wellspring clear.

Second, pour plenty of positive things into it. Philippians 4:8 says to think about things that are true, noble, right, pure, lovely, admirable, excellent, and worthy of praise. Ask the Holy Spirit to put on your heart the things that are on God's heart. There are many thirsty people in the world, so be sure to share this refreshing, life-giving living water, for you have plenty, and it is an *everlasting* spring.

JOURNAL THOUGHTS

What are some specific steps you can take to guard your heart this week?   .

memory verses

37

Above all else, guard your heart, for it is the wellspring of life.

PROVERBS 4:23

38

Whatever is true, whatever is noble, whatever is right, whatever is pure, whatever is lovely, whatever is admirable — if anything is excellent or praiseworthy — think about such things.

PHILIPPIANS 4:8

Holding on to a resentment was like eating rat poison and waiting for the rat to die.
ANNE LAMOTT, CROOKED LITTLE HEART

Stay alert; be in prayer so you don't wander into temptation without even knowing you're in danger. There is a part of you that is eager, ready for anything in God. But there's another part that's as lazy as an old dog sleeping by the fire.
MATTHEW 26:41, MSG

snakes in the garden

I was happily hiking in the woods near my house with my daughter and my dog. It was a gorgeous day and all seemed right with the world. Blue sky, singing birds, bright wildflowers sprinkled abundantly . . . perfect! All of a sudden, my daughter yelled from behind me, "Mom! Snake! Jump!"

At the same time I heard a hiss and a rattle near my ankle. I jumped and should have won a medal for height and distance. I looked back to see a very nasty looking old rattlesnake with several rattles, coiled and ready for action. His head turned and slanted eyes narrowed as he glared at me, showing his fangs. I never walked through that particular area again. It beckoned, but now I knew that it was deadly.

Our lives are like that. Satan is portrayed several times in the Bible as a serpent. Quiet, hidden, but deadly. He may not be obvious in your life, but he is there, biding his time.

After that day with the snake, I began wearing hiking boots instead of the more comfortable sport sandals I preferred. I wanted to be wise and protect myself.

Several times in my life, I have felt betrayed by people whom I had loved and trusted. I had a difficult time forgiving them. Anger, resentment, and self-pity began to eat into my soul. I should have heard the hissing sound at my feet. Eventually I did (God had to yell, "Snake! Jump!" really loud!). I saw how Satan was using the situation to inject poison into my soul and that of others. I asked God for forgiveness and for help to forgive. He was faithful. But I had to learn the hard way.

There are countless ways that Satan tries to bite and poison our soul. Envy, lust, busyness, selfishness, greed . . . the list of toxins is endless. Examine your heart regularly. Repenting includes the intent to turn and go another way. As someone said, if you don't want to fall down, don't walk in slippery places. You need to be alert, to know your points of weakness, and to ask God for protection. And listen for His timely warning: "Stop! Snake! Jump!"

JOURNAL THOUGHTS

Jot down one point of weakness you have and one way to stay alert and avoid this "snake."

memory verses

39

Whatever happens, conduct yourselves in a manner worthy of the gospel of Christ.

PHILIPPIANS 1:27

40

If we confess our sins, he is faithful and just and will forgive us our sins and purify us from all unrighteousness.

1 JOHN 1:9

God didn't leave any room for doubt when he told you how you should act when you got here. His example and the Commandments are plain enough, so just start there.

WILL ROGERS[1]

Therefore, there is now no condemnation for those who are in Christ Jesus.

ROMANS 8:1

starting over

Sometimes we just blow it. We mess up. Sin wins. The only remedy is to start over. Turn to God, who always gives second chances when we want to turn from our sins and change.

Ask God to help you look at your life with His eyes. Get rid of dead wood, broken glass, trash, weeds, and brambles. Clean out the junk. Eliminate the negative stuff in your soul garden. Now, again asking God's help, take inventory of what is left; what's the good stuff? Build on that.

Prepare the soil with prayer and a contrite heart. Next, consult with God on what His plan is for your life. Pick one thing from that plan. Maybe it's being more honest or loving, or being less critical; maybe it's forgiving someone.

You may feel it's a small thing, but go ahead, plant it, water it, nourish it from God's Word and ask God to make this new green thing in your life grow. Then stand back and thank Him for the new growth in your life. Have you ever gone to California and stood looking up at a giant sequoia tree? They started small too, but God gave them great potential.

Ask God to gather up all the old hurts, disappointments, regrets, and resentments in your life and use them for good, like mulch. Burn the diseased ones so they don't infect the rest of your life. Let God grow something new and beautiful in their place.

Journal Thoughts

Write down one area in which you need to grow. Ask God for forgiveness. Ask Him to change your attitude and actions, and to guide you in your growth.

memory verses

41

No temptation has seized you except what is common to man. And God is faithful; he will not let you be tempted beyond what you can bear. But when you are tempted, he will also provide a way out so that you can stand up under it.

1 CORINTHIANS 10:13

42

Create in me a pure heart, O God, and renew a steadfast spirit within me.

PSALM 51:10

week 22

Learn to say no; it will be of more use to you than to be able to read Latin.

CHARLES HADDON SPURGEON

Your enemy the devil prowls around like a roaring lion looking for someone to devour. Resist him.

1 PETER 5:8-9

poison ivy

When I was just beginning to learn about plants, I lived next door to an elderly widow. I decided to help her by cleaning up her yard. A great over-grown vine was choking a pretty yellow forsythia on one side of the yard; I began to tackle it. The sun was beating down and I wiped my face constantly as trickles of sweat glided down my skin. I finished grappling with the plant and packed it into several garbage bags.

My skin began to tingle, itch, and swell up into great red patches. Too late, I remembered the old saying about avoiding "shiny leaves of three." I scratched my skin and made it worse; every time I touched it, oil clung to my fingers and spread to a new spot. The doctor gave me shots, cream, and covered everything with gauze. I finally recovered, but now that I know what poison ivy looks like, you'd better believe I avoid it. The wind can carry it when burned, and pets carry the oil on their fur. So I don't even go near areas where it might grow.

Sin is just like poison ivy. It looks pretty harmless. Left alone it can turn into a towering vine that chokes the person it lives on. It's always the opposite of God's Word. It is harmful to people. The wounds it causes can spread to whomever touches it. It can be caught by spending time in its vicinity. Sin comes in many varieties, but they have some common characteristics. Learn to identify it so you can avoid it. If you cover it with prayer, repentance, and the balm of God's grace, He can heal it.

JOURNAL THOUGHTS

Write where you are the weakest regarding sin. Ask God to strengthen you and make you observant in ways to avoid temptation.

memory verses

43

Repent, then, and turn to God, so that your sins may be wiped out, that times of refreshing may come from the Lord.

ACTS 3:19

44

You are forgiving and good, O Lord, abounding in love to all who call to you.

PSALM 86:5

It is a great deal better to live a holy life than to talk about it. Lighthouses do not ring bells and fire cannon to call attention to their shining — they just shine.

Dwight L. Moody

Don't be so naive and self-confident. You're not exempt. You could fall flat on your face as easily as anyone else. Forget about self-confidence; it's useless. Cultivate God-confidence.

1 Corinthians 10:12, MSG

wild strawberries

There is nothing tastier than a wild raspberry. Hiking in the mountains on a hot day and coming upon some wild and unexpected fruit is a rare treat. On mountain hikes, even my dog would go up to the bushes and pull the snack off with his teeth, carefully avoiding the prickly thorns.

But in my garden, I have a real problem with wild berries. The bushes, unless constantly cut back, will grow into an impenetrable, impassable obstacle. The wild strawberry plants snake out hundreds of tiny tentacles that strangle any other plant in their path. I constantly have to guard the garden and keep ripping them out. I put in strong plants around them that can hold their own with tough roots.

Some people or interests in our lives act the same way. At first, they are fun, interesting, getting us into things that we ordinarily wouldn't experience. But like berries, they can be both sweet and tart. We can become ensnared in things that don't please God.

Sin has many innocent and tempting disguises. But anything that regularly pulls us away from the direction God wants us to go, we need to put entirely off limits. Become aware of the influences on your life, because whether it is sin or leads to sin, the principle is the same: You must control it before it grows to control you.

Plant strong, godly influences in your life. Make a pact with someone who holds you accountable. Find a godly mentor or be one. Don't underestimate the power of good Christian friends; spend time praying, reading, hearing, and memorizing the Bible. Then you can influence the people and things around you instead of being controlled by them. We are to be light in a dark world that needs so badly to hear and see Christ's love in our lives.

JOURNAL THOUGHTS

Write the name of someone you know who is struggling. Pray for them and do whatever you can to help.

memory verses

45

Though one may be overpowered, two can defend themselves. A cord of three strands is not quickly broken.

ECCLESIASTES 4:12

46

Do not be misled: "Bad company corrupts good character."

1 CORINTHIANS 15:33

They are the true disciples of Christ, not who know most, but who love most.

FREDERICH SPANHEIM THE ELDER

She who guards her mouth preserves her life, but she who opens wide her lips shall have destruction.

PROVERBS 13:3, PARAPHRASE

wasps

Every spring when the weather warms up, wasps come humming around our house. I have learned not to swat them for it only makes them mad and more determined. I like to garden chemical-free, but for wasps I get out the nasty poison spray and go a little crazy. I search out, scrape off, and destroy their nests. They are everywhere, and they frighten people when they buzz in their faces. I know they are supposed to be beneficial, but their sting is very hurtful. Unlike bees, which die once they sting, wasps can sting you and then fly away unaffected. They actually saw into your flesh with a serrated barb that goes deep into your skin.

Gossip is like that. It starts with one or two buzzing around, and then the group gets into it. Soon a barb goes into someone's skin and they are hurt. It saws into flesh. It can start innocently enough, even be disguised as sharing a prayer request. But we all know the difference. Things that are shared from the heart with a trusted friend for prayer are not to be given out as news to anyone else.

It's easy to fall into the habit. It seems like you are only sharing conversation. If there is a boss or someone else you dislike, you and your friends may all try to top one another with tales of things you have heard or seen. It may seem humorous when it is actually venomous. Perhaps a person made you angry, hurt you or someone you love, and you want to get even. It feels good to share that venom, but afterward you know that it was not innocent or funny, but poisonous. One good measure of whether something is gossip is if you would share the same thing if the person talked about were present. If you are ever in the vicinity of gossip, let others know you do not want anything to do with it, and leave. Make it a lifetime habit.

JOURNAL THOUGHTS

How can you avoid being involved in gossip?

memory verses

47

Take captive every thought to make it obedient to Christ.

2 CORINTHIANS 10:5

48

Set a guard over my mouth, O LORD; keep watch over the door of my lips. Let not my heart be drawn to what is evil.

PSALM 141:3-4

This indwelling Word keeps setting the trash by the door, keeps throwing open the windows to let in fresh air, and keeps leaving notes on the bathroom mirror—reminders to love, to trust, to give generously, to speak kindly.

JEAN FLEMING[2]

Wherewithal shall a young [woman] cleanse [her] way? By taking heed thereto according to thy word. . . . Thy word have I hid in mine heart, that I might not sin against thee.

PSALM 119:9,11, KJV

stop weeds before they start!

Weeds. They need to be prevented before they grow up quickly and choke out the good plants. Some of them actually curl around the throat of other plants and choke them to death. All it takes for weeds to grow is some loose, empty soil and inattention from the gardener. Putting off pulling weeds for even a day helps them spread as their roots take hold, making them more difficult to get rid of. You need a sharp spade or a pronged weed digger and some strong weed killer. Some organic gardeners use strong vinegar and salt.

Jesus told a story about a farmer who had sown good seed. But an enemy had sown weeds, and soon they came up and choked the good plants. Jesus explained that the field was the world, the good sower was the Son of Man, and the enemy was the Devil. Satan loves to hide weeds in good soil, let them germinate, and wait for the surprise.

God hates sin, but He will not do the weeding for you. He is stronger than evil and lends you His strength if you ask. Don't let Satan sneak sin into your life disguised as something harmless. Use the sharp edges of the Word of God to dig out sin as soon as it rears its ugly head. Plant good things in its place. Keep God's Word in your heart. Grow strong fruit in your life that leaves no room for sin.

Ask Christ to shield you from temptation and pour His grace on you. God loves you, no matter how many times you blow it. Just keep obeying His Word. "The word of God is living and powerful, and sharper than any two-edged sword, piercing even to the division of soul and spirit, and of joints and marrow, and is a discerner of the thoughts and intents of the heart." (Hebrews 4:12, NKJV)

JOURNAL THOUGHTS

Is there a persistent sin in your life that you can't seem to get rid of? Make a plan with God to get rid of it. Ask a trusted friend for prayer.

memory verses

49
Fight the good fight.
1 TIMOTHY 1:18

50
Submit yourselves, then, to God. Resist the devil, and he will flee from you.
JAMES 4:7

Every Christian who makes progress in holiness is a person who has disciplined his life so that he spends regular time in the Bible. There simply is no other way.

JERRY BRIDGES, *THE PURSUIT OF HOLINESS*

I am the true vine, and my Father is the gardener. He cuts away every branch of mine that doesn't produce fruit. But he trims clean every branch that does produce fruit, so that it will produce even more fruit. Stay joined to me, and I will stay joined to you. Just as a branch cannot produce fruit unless it stays joined to the vine, you cannot produce fruit unless you stay joined to me.

JOHN 15:1-2,4, CEV

pruning

I remember the first time I saw my father prune something. There were two beautiful, large flowering shrubs in the corner of our backyard. I wanted to grab his pruners and stop him. I was afraid he would kill them or make them so small and weak they would never be the large and beautiful shrubs I had loved. But he kept cutting. And in the spring, those plants were glorious. New growth sprang from what had been dead and overgrown. There were twice as many blooms. The fragrance filled the air and bees buzzed, deliriously content within the branches.

God cares for us, so He regularly does some pruning in our lives. Let Him choose the branches. He carefully keeps what is essential and burns the junk. He cuts off the things in our lives that don't bear fruit. Pruning is painful but feels good later when the dead and diseased branches are gone from our lives. Sometimes we want our Father to stop, but we must trust Him.

Good things that are not fruitful or in the right timing in your life may have to go. Trust Christ. Allow His nail-scarred hands to wield the pruners generously. In God's time, the beauty of new growth in your life will be glorious and the sweet aroma of Christ will draw many to Him.

JOURNAL THOUGHTS

Jot down one area of your life that needs pruning. Ask God to produce healthy fruit and good growth in that area.

memory verses

51

Whoever claims to live in him must walk as Jesus did.

1 JOHN 2:6

52

I have come that they may have life, and have it to the full.

JOHN 10:10

part 5:

growing in love

I have learned in my years on earth to hold everything loosely, because when I hold things tightly, God has to pry my fingers away. And that hurts.

CORRIE TEN BOOM, *CLIPPINGS FROM MY NOTEBOOK*

Let the thirsty ones come — anyone who wants to.
Let them come and drink the water of life without charge.

REVELATION 22:17, NLT

love is like zucchini

Squash. Zucchini! Need I say more? Even if you have never gardened before, just stick a few seeds in a sunny place and wait for the explosion. Zucchini amazes children and adults alike. The stuff is good! But everyone who has ever grown them has had to become very creative with the bounty of their harvest. Neighbors share nutritious recipes for breads and casseroles. Some women load zucchini into bags and shove their husbands and children out the door with the admonishment to not return until the last veggie is gone. Baskets full of green squash mysteriously appear on doorsteps and in office eating areas, labeled "Free! Take as many as you want!"

God's love and grace is like that. It is free and there is an endless supply. Sometimes we act like there isn't enough grace to go around. We unconsciously think if we give grace, love, or forgiveness to someone else, somehow we won't have enough. We hoard love and approval. But love is like zucchini. There will always be plenty to share. Christians are blessed with an overflowing bounty for one reason: We are to share it with a needy world.

JOURNAL THOUGHTS

Here are some extra verses. There was such a surplus I had to share them. Enjoy.

For you know the grace of our Lord Jesus Christ, that though he was rich, yet for your sakes he became poor, so that you through his poverty might become rich.

2 CORINTHIANS 8:9

Dear friends, since God so loved us, we also ought to love one another.

1 JOHN 4:11

memory verses

53

Freely you have received, freely give.

MATTHEW 10:8

54

Watch out! Be on your guard against all kinds of greed; a [woman's] life does not consist in the abundance of [her] possessions.

LUKE 12:15

When our God, who is Mercy, comes like a shout into your darkness, when the Father stoops down and tenderly picks up the pieces of your broken life, when Jesus steps in front of what you could have deserved, and when the Lord of heaven says, "I still want you," after you thought no one would, it is the most amazing truth of all. I have been over-whelmed by this lavish kingdom gift called mercy.

ANGELA THOMAS, *A BEAUTIFUL OFFERING*

For I was hungry and you fed me, thirsty and you gave me a drink, a stranger and you asked me in, ragged and you clothed me, sick and you cared for me, in prison and you vis-ited me . . . I tell you that whatever you did for the least of these, my brothers and sisters, you did for me.

MATTHEW 25:35-36,40, PARAPHRASE

winding paths

There is a children's story about a man who wanted to be a knight. He desired to do great and mighty things for his king. He went on a long, winding journey to appear before the king for the knighting ceremony. Along the way, people kept asking him for help. At first, he helped mere-ly to get them out of his way, but slowly his heart began to change. He began to understand their needs and love them. As the long journey con-tinued, the knight spent so much time helping others that he was poor, old, and worn-out by the time he finally met the king. He felt unworthy, with nothing left to offer. But the king knighted him because his life had been given for others, which was a knight's true duty.

As Christians, what does our King require us to do? "To act justly and to love mercy and to walk humbly with your God" (Micah 6:8). Our path on earth is a meandering one. We pass by cool streams and green meadows. We also go by dirty alleys, burning houses, and people in need. As children of God, we are to act justly, to show mercy and compassion along our journey. We are to do it joyfully, not as a duty. If we know and love God, the things that are on His heart will be on ours.

How many times have we been guilty of gritting our teeth or checking our watch while helping someone? Sometimes, when we help others, we secretly begrudge them the time from our busy schedule or resent their need. Our natural desire is to focus on ourselves. As God so lavishly gave us mercy, we need to give mercy to others. When we are Christ-centered, not self-centered, service becomes joyful. It is through giving that we receive. God loves a cheerful giver (2 Corinthians 9:7).

Christ showed us, over and over, how to serve. Thank God for the gifts He has given you so that you have something to share, whether it is time, money, service, or just a kind word and touch. Live to be joyfully worn-out in His service, like that long-ago knight.

JOURNAL THOUGHTS

Describe the heart of a servant.

memory verses

55

And what does the LORD require of you? To act justly and to love mercy and to walk humbly with your God.

MICAH 6:8

56

Be completely humble and gentle; be patient, bearing with one another in love.

EPHESIANS 4:2

Always tell of God's love. If necessary, use words.

ST. FRANCIS OF ASSISI

Now that I, your Lord and Teacher, have washed your feet, you also should wash one another's feet. I have set you an example that you should do as I have done for you.

JOHN 13:14-15

get down to earth

Mud. We avoid it if at all possible. Christians are sometimes known for steering clear of messy situations. Whenever there is an untidy divorce or someone steps into obvious, muddy sin that cannot be ignored, we frequently fall short in the loving, washing dirty feet department.

If a friend has a sin problem, it may seem to put too much of a strain on our relationship. Instead of confronting them in love and walking through it with them, we may run away from the whole thing. We may be too busy trying to keep our own lives going well to stop and pick up a neighbor who is doing less than well. Or we feel inadequate to help, so we pass them by on the other side of the supermarket aisle.

Jesus washed muddy feet and sat down to meals with friends who were sinners. Let's obey and follow His example. Have a friend with muddy feet? Kneel down and wash them. Think of what you would need most in their place. We can hold a hand, lend assistance, share a tear, share a prayer, share money or time, point the way to counsel, but most of all, remain constant in Christian love. Our responsibility is not to fix their problem but to walk with them in love. Jesus Christ loved us and died for you and me, even though we were muddy sinners. Christ commands us to love one another, even when it's a dirty job.

JOURNAL THOUGHTS

Reflect on how you respond to people in your life with "muddy feet."

memory verses

57

Above all, love each other deeply, because love covers over a multitude of sins.

1 PETER 4:8

58

A friend loves at all times, and a [sister] is born for adversity.

PROVERBS 17:17

Because purpose flows out of our relationship with God, our purposes are part of our spiritual journey. . . . As God leads us into a life of greater trust, integrity, and selflessness, doors will open and we'll be equipped for tasks that once scared us.

JAN JOHNSON, *LIVING A PURPOSE-FULL LIFE*

Love one another deeply, from the heart.

1 PETER 1:22

new varieties

Every year my parents liked to try something new in their garden. They had old favorites, but they enjoyed going down the crowded rows in the nursery, looking for new varieties to try. Maybe a new type of tomato or a different color for the window boxes. They did the same thing at the supermarket, trying a new fruit or vegetable that they had never tasted. In their eighties, they are still adventurous and open to new experiences.

When I was young, I had a personal code: When in doubt, do it. This meant that if I had a choice of whether to become involved in something good, from going on a trip to entering graduate school, that unless there were very definite reasons for *not* doing something (sin, godly counsel, priorities, time, and so on) I would choose to do it. I wanted to take wise risks. I didn't want to look back on my life with a lot of regret for staying uninvolved. The times I violated that rule and played it safe or lazy, I regretted it because I missed God's best for my life.

We have a vastly creative God who wants our time on earth to be worthwhile. Look at the countless wild adventures of people in the Bible and others in the past who said "yes" to God. Look at all the needs met, people helped, missions started, the good news about God's love shared all over the world. All because people were willing to leave their comfort zone and try something new. This doesn't mean that you have to travel out of your hometown . . . or it may mean traveling the earth.

Don't stand on the sidelines and watch. Dig in. Be part of the messi-ness of life. Exercise your faith. God has a personal plan for each of us that uses all the capabilities He has given us. Focus in on what really counts . . . love God and love people. That's pretty much it. God is talking to you. Have an adventure and say "Yes!"

JOURNAL THOUGHTS

Reflect on a time you've said "yes" to God. What kind of adventure and growth followed?
Ask God to give you a new opportunity to serve Him.

memory verses

59

Whatever your hand finds to do, do it with all your might.

ECCLESIASTES 9:10

60

Let us not become weary in doing good, for at the proper time we will reap a harvest
if we do not give up. Therefore, as we have opportunity, let us do good to all people,
especially to those who belong to the family of believers.

GALATIANS 6:9-10

Do not wait for leaders. Do it alone, person to person.

MOTHER TERESA

But all of you, leaders and followers alike, are to be down to earth with each other, for — "God has had it with the proud, but takes delight in just plain people." So be content with who you are, and don't put on airs. God's strong hand is on you; he'll promote you at the right time. Live carefree before God; he is most careful with you.

1 PETER 5:5-7, MSG

marigolds

Cheerful, undemanding, reliable, unceasing in production.

Humble marigolds. They're very common. Everyone has a few in their garden because they are so bright, dependable, and cheerful. But few people pick them for a beautiful bouquet because they're small and plain and have a slightly musty scent. Yet they serve good purposes. Marigolds keep bugs and other critters away from the other plants in the garden. They border the large, showy flowers. They're easy to grow, and they bloom their little heads off without a lot of fuss.

Marigold people. They are the cheerful quiet ones who often serve unnoticed and overlooked. They staff the church nursery. They serve for small pay and little praise. They are the dependable ones. If something needs to be done, they do it. Often they don't have money for cool clothes or the latest stuff. Dig into their lives and you'll find they've been helping someone financially: a niece that needed funds for school, elderly parents, or a brother with health problems. They do the tough jobs that no one else wants to do, like planning and cleaning up after events. They help single moms or poorly paid parents by babysitting for free. They work with foster children, the physically and mentally handicapped, and the homeless. They spend time with unruly teens in trouble with the law. They walk or run in events to raise money for charity. They come alongside people who need an encouraging word.

When Jesus talked about being humble, like a child, we all nod our heads yes. He cleaned and cooked fish for His disciples. He washed their dirty feet. But only a few of us wash feet without wanting our picture in the paper for it. Only a few of us serve quietly in the background with a genuine smile because we see Jesus in others. We forget how humble Jesus was. He was God but became human and gave away all His power and right to be worshiped. He rode on a donkey instead of in a king's chariot. After He washed our feet, He loved us enough to die on the cross.

The next time you see a marigold, remember: We are to serve others like Jesus did. Quietly, joyfully, doing the tough jobs that God equipped us to do.

JOURNAL THOUGHTS

List the "marigold people" in your life who have helped you, then make it a point to thank them. Look for a place to serve where only you and God will know about it.

memory verses

61

Dear children, let us not love with words or tongue but with actions and in truth.

1 JOHN 3:18

62

The entire law is summed up in a single command: "Love your neighbor as yourself."

GALATIANS 5:14

Joy is the echo of God's life within us.

JOSEPH MARMION, ORTHODOXY

Love must be sincere. Hate what is evil; cling to what is good. Be devoted to one another in brotherly love. Honor one another above yourselves. . . . Be joyful in hope, patient in affliction, faithful in prayer.

ROMANS 12:9-10,12

miracle grow

Encourages strong growth, beautiful blooms, and fruit.

I always had trouble growing a garden in the mountains until I stumbled on a wonderful product, Miracle-Gro. You just dissolve this green powder in water and wonderful things happen. I soak the dry roots of plants in the green water before I plant them. Throughout the summer, I try to give the garden a weekly bath of the mixture. The plants just perk up and bloom. I swear I can almost see them smiling and hear tiny little burps when they get their weekly green juice.

The Bible teaches us that pleasant words, love, joy, and laughter do the same for people as Miracle-Gro does for plants. It says that merry hearts help people heal just like medicine. Paul talked a lot about joy. He didn't confuse it with happiness. This was a guy who was often beaten for being a Christian but who sang when chained up in prison. A merry heart, regardless of personal circumstances. Where does that kind of joy come from? It comes from experiencing the love of God. It comes from living a life of faith. It comes from our position as beloved children of God. The God who cared enough to suffer, forgive, and die for our sins on a wooden cross on a hill. The God who walks with us. The very same God who lives as our protector and our hope, who will take us home with Him someday.

If our words help people grow and bloom, like Miracle-Gro does for plants, why do we withhold them? Try to share an encouraging word with someone every day. Pick a person or a place that could use some cheer. Figure out a way to share the joy of Christ with a merry heart. Start with the people closest to you.

JOURNAL THOUGHTS

Think about what you've just read. Are you experiencing joy in your life? If not, you can't share it. Reflect on ways to allow more joy in your life. If Paul could have joy in prison chains, God can do the same for you.

memory verses

63

Pleasant words are a honeycomb, sweet to the soul and healing to the bones.
PROVERBS 16:24

64

Though the fig tree does not bud and there are no grapes on the vines, though the olive crop fails and the fields produce no food, though there are no sheep in the pen and no cattle in the stalls, yet I will rejoice in the LORD, I will be joyful in God my Savior. The Sovereign LORD is my strength.
HABAKKUK 3:17-19

God has given us two hands — one to receive with and the other to give with.
We are not cisterns made for hoarding; we are channels made for sharing.

BILLY GRAHAM

Let us not love in theory or in speech but in deed and in truth.

1 JOHN 3:18, AMP

garden angels

I keep a small, stone angel in my garden as a reminder to help strangers. I'm not always grace-filled when strangers intrude in my life. How do you react when strangers enter into your space? The space in your office? The space in front of you on the freeway? Your personal space anytime, anywhere? Even our families can make us irritable if we have not had personal private time alone and with God, a time of renewal.

The world is too close today. The media searches and finds terrible things happening in every far corner of the world. We become overwhelmed. Since we cannot help or fix all these things happening to strangers, we may develop a thin hard shell of indifference as protection. Maybe we ignore strangers in our midst because it's easier, or we don't have time, or we are selfish. We begin to cross the street when confronted by a stranger in need. It is bit by bit, with small cruelties and coldness that we gradually lose our sensitivity to the needs of others and forfeit our sense of community.

It's hard to love others. But God loved us while we were unrepentant, unlovely sinners, strangers to His love. Ask God to keep your heart warm toward strangers in our bitterly cold world. Christ told us to love our neighbor as we love ourselves. He taught that our neighbor is anyone in need. Love toward strangers is an act of obedience we can give to God as a gift. And, in sharing God's grace with strangers, we may unwittingly be spending time with angels. "Do not forget to entertain strangers, for by so doing some people have entertained angels without knowing it" (Hebrews 13:2).

JOURNAL THOUGHTS

Write one or two ways you could use your gifts or blessings to help a stranger. Ask God to give you opportunities to pass His love on to strangers.

memory verses

65

Be wise in the way you act toward outsiders; make the most of every opportunity. Let your conversation be always full of grace, seasoned with salt, so that you may know how to answer everyone.

COLOSSIANS 4:5-6

66

"Love the Lord your God with all your heart and with all your soul and with all your mind." This is the first and greatest commandment. And the second is like it: "Love your neighbor as yourself."

MATTHEW 22:37-39

Of all earthly music, that which reaches farthest into heaven is the beating of a truly loving heart.

Henry Ward Beecher

Blessed is the [woman] who trusts in the LORD, whose confidence is in him. [She] will be like a tree planted by the water that sends out its roots by the stream. It does not fear when heat comes; its leaves are always green. It has no worries in a year of drought and never fails to bear fruit.

Jeremiah 17:7-8

sweet fragrance of Christ

What kind of a fragrance have you been giving off lately? And I don't mean your perfume. Have you ever gotten in your car, driven down the highway, and totally lost your cool? Rude drivers cut us off and we either retaliate or say and think rude things about them. I have to use a combination of prayer, repeating Scripture verses, and muttering, "I will not let other drivers dictate the way I drive." Sometimes I call people jerks and compare their intelligence to that of a garden slug. I have a long list of sins — "road rudeness" is just one of many.

Yet God says we are to be the "aroma of Christ" to others. How are we, imperfect and fully human Christians, supposed to daily muster enough love to spread a sweet fragrance in the world?

The answer is, Christ in me. I am most prone to sin and least able to love when I have not spent regular time with Christ, breathing His sweet aroma, listening to His Holy Spirit. Studying the Bible, praying throughout my day, reading Christian books, worshiping in church, or spending time talking about life's trials with encouraging Christian friends all help. These regular habits of spending time with Christ fill me with the sweet fragrance of Christ's love and grace. When I spend too much time with the world, I begin to smell like the world, with a whiff of burning sulfur and garbage. Like cigarette smoke, the world can permeate life.

Think of the fragrance of your favorite flower. Place it in your mind; you can almost smell it. If we are to give off the sweet fragrance of Christ, we need to spend time with Him. Then we who have been given and forgiven so much will bring the fresh scent of life, love, and forgiveness to a world dying in the polluted stench of sin and Satan. They will know we are Christians by our love.

JOURNAL THOUGHTS

What kind of fragrance have you been sharing lately?

memory verses

67

We love because he first loved us.

I JOHN 4:19

68

For we are to God the aroma of Christ among [the saved and the perishing]. To the one we are the smell of death; to the other the fragrance of life. . . . Not that we are competent in ourselves to claim anything for ourselves, but our competence comes from God.

2 CORINTHIANS 2:15-16; 3:5

part 6:

growing in wisdom

Our minds are transformed when we apply our thoughts to things
that cause transformation.

KAREN O'CONNOR, *BASKET OF BLESSINGS*

Wisdom is a shelter as money is a shelter, but the advantage of knowledge is this:
that wisdom preserves the life of its possessor.

ECCLESIASTES 7:12

follow the instructions

A sure sign of spring is the appearance of the little wire racks in the super-
markets filled with small, bright packages of promise. New packets of
flower and vegetable seeds. Little packages of hope. I love to read them
and envision all the wonderful things that could, if given enough time,
energy, perseverance, and hard work, grow in my garden.

The photos on the front of the pack are beautiful and enticing. But
the important part is the small print on the back: the planting instructions. Without them, you might as well just throw your money and seeds
away into the wind. The directions come from an authority who knows
the plant and exactly what it needs to get a good start and thrive. No one
would buy the seeds and ignore the instructions, or decide they knew better than the expert who designed the package. The instructions are complete and precise. Soil depth, closeness of plants, type of location, type of
soil, and on and on. Often, they add an 800-number hotline for any
questions.

If we are the seed, God's Word contains the instructions for our life. They are complete and precise. They are intended to let us thrive in the best conditions for our maximum growth. He has given us the Holy Spirit as a hotline for more direction. God promises to instruct, teach, counsel, and watch over you (Psalm 32:8). Who knows us better than our Maker? Seek His will for your life. Read His instructions and follow them.

JOURNAL THOUGHTS

Ask God today for personal direction. Spend some time in Proverbs, reading His instructions.

memory verses

69

Call to me and I will answer you and tell you great and unsearchable things you do not know.

JEREMIAH 33:3

70

If any of you lacks wisdom, [she] should ask God, who gives generously to all without finding fault, and it will be given to [her].

JAMES 1:5

Love is not blind — it sees more, not less. But because it sees more, it is willing to see less.
RABBI JULIUS GORDON

And this is love: that we walk in obedience to his commands. As you have heard from the beginning, his command is that you walk in love.
2 JOHN 1:6

boundaries

Setting out stakes for a garden marks off the places for which you will be responsible. If there are weeds or rocks or sandy soil in other parts of the yard, that is not your responsibility. Imagine trying to garden with no boundary markers. The task would be endless and impossible. Your garden would extend to the state line and beyond. You would be stretched beyond your capabilities, do a poor job, and keep other people from working and growing because it all belongs to you.

Sometimes people have a hard time setting boundaries. You gradually take on more and more, for diverse reasons. Finally, you are struggling under a heavy load you were not meant to carry. You may take on the sorrows of a friend, work conflicts, the problems of a grown child, the character flaws of a mate or a sibling, feeding and caring for the homeless, or any of the many problems and social ills of your world. All of these things are good, but where do you stop? What are the things God wants you to do? A wise person learns to focus on the specific areas God gives them and set firm boundaries.

When my husband and I were young, we were approached by a Christian mission organization about a full-time assignment. We had just returned from a two-year military term in Europe, and my desire was to stay near family. I was scared but willing to go where God wanted us. The next day we learned our destination was a university just a two-hour drive from family and friends. God knew me. As a young woman of small and yet untested faith, He knew just how far I could be stretched.

Why are we so surprised when God demonstrates that He *knows* us, inside and out? God made you. God loves you and has a *perfect* plan for your life. That doesn't mean all of life will be pleasant; it does mean God has personally tailored your life to use everything in it to produce the best that you can be. He knows your passions, your heart, and your gifts. Can you trust Him to set your boundaries?

JOURNAL THOUGHTS

Reflect on the present boundaries in your life. Do any stakes need to be moved farther out or closer in?

memory verses

71

Come to me, all you who are weary and burdened, and I will give you rest. Take my yoke upon you and learn from me, for I am gentle and humble in heart, and you will find rest for your souls. For my yoke is easy and my burden is light.

MATTHEW 11:28-30

72

But those who hope in the LORD will renew their strength. They will soar on wings like eagles; they will run and not grow weary, they will walk and not be faint.

ISAIAH 40:31

There were no formerly heroic times and there was no formerly pure generation. . . .
There is no one here but us chickens, and so it always has been. . . . There never was a
more holy age than ours, and never a less. There is no less holiness at this time — as you
are reading this — than there was the day the Red Sea parted.

ANNIE DILLARD, *FOR THE TIME BEING*

It is not that we think we can do anything of lasting value by ourselves.
Our only power and success come from God.

2 CORINTHIANS 3:5, NLT

burning bushes

Burning bush is one of my favorite plants. It is so brilliant you can't miss
it. That's the way I wish God would always speak to me. A large, burning
billboard would be even better. But He does still speak to us, especially in
the Bible. Reading through the Bible, we may get the idea that the people
in it were somehow different from us, more holy than us. They got to see
burning bushes and a parted sea, angels spoke to them, and some of them
actually walked and ate and talked with Jesus. But if you read on, you see
that even with all that, they still messed up, they grumbled, and they
sinned by going their own way in spite of God's advice. So, they weren't
very different from us after all.

Peter is one of my favorite disciples. He was always rushing ahead,
putting his foot in his mouth, grabbing for Jesus' attention. But he loved
Jesus fervently; he wanted so much to have His approval. He messed up

colossally but he also loved gigantically. He didn't do anything halfheartedly. He was not a lukewarm disciple. He desperately wanted to understand the heart of God.

Someone asked me what I thought about a theological controversy that was all the current rage at the time. I answered truthfully that if I could just get the basics down first, like loving my neighbor, maybe I could progress to thinking about more complex issues. There are so many simple commands God gave us (they're pretty much on a burning billboard) that we can spend a lifetime working on them with God's grace. Pay attention to the burning bush in your own yard and God will give you plenty of direction. As you obey Him in the obvious, you, like Peter, will begin to understand the heart of God.

JOURNAL THOUGHTS

How can you walk justly, love mercy, and walk humbly with your God this week?

memory verses

73

I pray that you, being rooted and established in love, may have power, together with all the saints, to grasp how wide and long and high and deep is the love of Christ.

EPHESIANS 3:17-18

74

Stand at the crossroads and look; ask for the ancient paths, ask where the good way is, and walk in it, and you will find rest for your souls.

JEREMIAH 6:16

Temptation, at its core, is a shortcut . . . the fast track to quick results. Satan's strategy against Christians usually suggests we do three things: move quickly, think shallowly, and invest ourselves deeply. But . . . the reward is short-term and the consequences are long-term.

RON MEHL, SURPRISE ENDINGS[1]

This is for keeps, a life-or-death fight to the finish against the Devil and all his angels. Be prepared. . . . Take all the help you can get.

EPHESIANS 6:12-13, MSG

cold-hardy cacti

Why do some plants make it through the most severe winters while others die at the first kiss of frost? Cold-hardy plants are just as fragile on the inside; they have the same root system and delicate flowers. But they are hardy on the outside. They have a sort of plant armor that protects them and allows them to keep coming back after severe attacks of bad weather. Storms actually encourage their roots to grow deeper. They stand up well to adversity.

One example is the Royal Gorge Spiney Hedgehog, a small blooming cactus in Colorado that endures hot, dry summers and bone-chilling winters. It takes years of growth before it blooms, but by then it is strong and established. (Note: Be patient with yourself and other late bloomers.) Its spiney armor lets it stand up to anything short of a bulldozer.

God wants Christians to be well-protected. He sends storms to strengthen our resistance and offers us spiritual armor. He doesn't want us going into battle unprotected, but some of us insist on showing up in "Friday casual" jeans and sandals. Then, when we are wounded, we wonder why God didn't protect us. Well, we made the decision to leave our armor in the closet!

Life is full of choices. As pastor and author Ron Mehl put it, "Life is made of little turnings, little decisions. It is folly to think we can continually turn one way in all our small decisions and then tell ourselves we'll do differently when the big matters come along."[1]

Whether we realize it or not, we are in a constant, daily battle with evil. The images of evil in movies such as *Harry Potter* or *The Lord of the Rings* pale in comparison with reality. Satan is hideous, but he masquerades as an angel of beauty and light; he plays music to the world that entices it to dance to the tune of selfishness.

Every time you go to God in prayer, read and memorize His Word, follow the leading of the Spirit, step out in faith, stand for righteousness, share the good news of grace and forgiveness, or make a decision to do something God's way, you put one more square of armored plate on for defense. Ultimately, the Lord is our strength and our defender, but He wants you strong, mature, and equipped to stand against evil — not weak and buffeted by every ill wind that blows.

Examine your daily habits and your small decisions. Are they building you up? When things get tough do you cut and run or make a stand with God? God gives you small daily battles so you will be prepared to stand and win when really tough things come into your life.

JOURNAL THOUGHTS

Read Ephesians 6. Examine your habits. What do you need to do to be better prepared for spiritual battle?

memory verses

75

For God did not give us a spirit of timidity, but a spirit of power, of love and of self-discipline.

2 TIMOTHY 1:7

76

Stand firm then, with the belt of truth buckled around your waist, with the breast-plate of righteousness in place, and with your feet fitted with the readiness that comes from the gospel of peace. In addition to all this, take up the shield of faith, with which you can extinguish all the flaming arrows of the evil one. Take the helmet of salvation and the sword of the Spirit, which is the word of God.

EPHESIANS 6:14-17

Wisdom is the acquired ability to live life well. It's living life against the grindstone and coming away polished instead of being chewed up.

DAVID SWARTZ, *DANCING WITH BROKEN BONES*

Jesus said . . . "Why are you bothering this woman? She has done a beautiful thing to me . . . I tell you the truth, wherever this gospel is preached throughout the world, what she has done will also be told, in memory of her."

MATTHEW 26:10,13

beauty in pansy faces

One of the happiest flowers is the common pansy. Pansies have bright painted faces, turned up and smiling at everyone who passes by. They come in all sorts of lovely color combinations. They are also extremely sturdy; they're the first up in the cold spring. Pansies spread and keep coming up by themselves for years. They don't require any fancy care. They're beautiful, but they don't get by on their beauty alone.

What is beauty? Artificial beauty is all on the surface: pretty clothes, good hair and makeup, straight white teeth. True beauty comes from the heart; it is a combination of love and strength of character.

The most beautiful women I know have been through the toughest times and triumphed, like the pansies pushing through the snow. Some are single mothers, who for varied reasons ended up raising their children alone. Some are widows who have begun their lives a second time. Some are single women who have no permanent home but travel the world dedicated to ministry. Some are moms with foster or adopted children no one wanted. Others run businesses but are always helping others. There are busy wives and mothers who always seek out people who need a caring touch.

They are certainly not perfect. They struggle; they get tired and discouraged just like the rest of us. But several things are common to all of these beautiful women. They have an "attitude of gratitude" toward God and others. They choose not to focus on what they do not have. They focus on the needs of others. They encourage others. They radiate joy and contentment versus mere happiness. They love and know they are loved by God. They serve God and people with an eternal perspective.

The most important thing they have in common is that they put God first. They spend time with Him and His Word. They reflect Him in their faces. They trust Him and rest in that trust. Want to become more beautiful? Spend some time with the God who loves you.

Journal Thoughts

Describe a godly woman you admire. Ask God to make you more beautiful from the inside out.

memory verses

77

Am I now trying to win the approval of men, or of God? Or am I trying to please men? If I were still trying to please men, I would not be a servant of Christ.

GALATIANS 1:10

78

Charm is deceptive, and beauty is fleeting; but a woman who fears the LORD is to be praised.

PROVERBS 31:30

part 7:

growing in joy

Take back the day. Stop your work — and stop thinking about your work.
Clear your mind. Calm your spirit. Bless the children.
Worship, meditate, pray, nap, walk, enjoy nature.

RICHARD A. SWENSON, M.D., *A MINUTE OF MARGIN*

As the deer pants for streams of water, so my soul pants for you, O God.

PSALM 42:1

a deep well

I live in the West, which has been experiencing a bad drought. All the communities around us have strict watering rules for lawns and gardens. There is no watering allowed between 9 AM and 5 PM, along with many other restrictions. Some of the wells in the outlying areas have begun to go dry, so people have to truck water in from other places. People are concerned, because without water there is no life.

The people in biblical times were more aware than we are of the value of water. Many of them were desert nomads, who could only pitch their tents where there was abundant water for them and their animals. People in cities dug deep wells to share. When precious water ran out in the cities, it had to be carried in and sold in clay pots. That's one reason Jesus talked about water so much. People understood that it was life-giving.

While climbing in the mountains, you often see a lone tree or shrub, growing out of a rock or a cliff. It looks strange, as though it is growing out of barren hardness. But the roots are indescribably strong, going deep, into underground streams.

Women in exercise classes routinely drink water from bottles they carry with them because their bodies crave water to function well. Our bodies are more than 90 percent water. Without water, we would collapse. Once we understand the importance of water, we begin to comprehend the profound necessity of pausing and filling up regularly from the Spring of Life.

The story of Mary and Martha illustrates this. Martha invited Jesus to her home and was preparing a fancy meal but her sister Mary paused. She sat at Jesus' feet and listened to Him. She filled up her spirit with Living Water. Jesus said Mary had chosen to do the only thing that was really necessary.

Make a regular habit of spending time just enjoying Jesus and the Father. Maybe it's taking a prayer walk, praying with a friend, quiet time reading a fresh translation of the Bible, or extended private time in prayer and meditation. Whatever your soul needs, don't go too long without Him. Take action. Without water, there is no life.

JOURNAL THOUGHTS

What refreshes your soul?

memory verses

79

If [a woman] is thirsty, let [her] come to me and drink. Whoever believes in me, as the Scripture has said, streams of living water will flow from within [her].

JOHN 7:37-38

80

I am the Alpha and the Omega, the Beginning and the End. To [her] who is thirsty I will give to drink without cost from the spring of the water of life.

REVELATION 21:6

Love is more than a characteristic of God; it is His character.

ANONYMOUS

I am still confident of this: I will see the goodness of the LORD in the land of the living.

PSALM 27:13

winter hope

Snow is falling on the garden, rendering it almost invisible. The dark, bare sticks of shrubs look lifeless, but they will be covered in green in the spring. I know that underneath, the bulbs and roots and rich soil are still there, waiting for the warm weather and sunshine, when they will flower once more. The cheery daffodils and crocus will pop up and make me smile. I know, yet my soul is sad and gloomy like the dark and bone-chilling weather.

Maybe you have had times of winter lately. Disappointment in love, losing a loved one to death or severe illness, not getting a job you really wanted, even the death of a beloved pet; the list is long and affects us all. Sometimes it's just a feeling of unworthiness coming from an action of our own, where we let someone down or didn't do something well.

We all have periods of hopelessness and sadness that seem like a long winter to our souls. It's part of living. How do we make it till spring, while winter's wind is still sweeping through our souls? How do we light a cozy fire to warm and cheer us deep down inside?

Times of winter in our lives are times when we can rely more on God.

Give your troubles to Him and leave them there. Ask Him where you should focus your energy. Many people who have been diagnosed with life-threatening illnesses have said that it was one of the best things that ever happened to them. It caused them to slow down and really focus in on what was important in life.

We all are finite but we sometimes act like we will live on this earth forever. We need to make the most of every day; our choices need to be made in accordance with God's plan for our lives. Don't waste another minute. Prioritize the people and the things God has planned for you, and make every day count. "Pile your troubles on GOD's shoulders — he'll carry your load, he'll help you out" (Psalm 55:22, MSG). And, as He planned, the crocus and daffodils will show their cheery heads and we *will* smile again. Every winter carries the promise of spring.

JOURNAL THOUGHTS

Read Psalm 27. Write down your thoughts on finding peace in the midst of trouble or sorrow.

memory verses

81

You will keep in perfect peace [her] whose mind is steadfast, because [she] trusts in you.

ISAIAH 26:3

82

But I will sing of your strength, in the morning I will sing of your love; for you are my fortress, my refuge in times of trouble.

PSALM 59:16

If you have no joy in your religion, there's a leak in your Christianity somewhere.

W. A. "BILLY" SUNDAY

GOD, my shepherd! I don't need a thing. You have bedded me down in lush meadows, you find me quiet pools to drink from. True to your word, you let me catch my breath and send me in the right direction.

PSALM 23:1-3, MSG

resting in the shadow

As a child, growing up in Ohio, there was nothing better than sitting on the screened-in porch on a summer evening. All you could hear were soft birdcalls. The mosquitoes couldn't get in and the fireflies would start their show, blinking on and off all over the yard. Murmurs of adults talking over their day were soothing reassurance in the background. The rhythmic squeak of the porch swing moving back and forth was hypnotizing. We could all just sit back and relax.

Throughout the Bible people speak of God restoring their soul. What does that mean? Dr. Richard Swenson, writing in *A Minute of Margin*, says God gave us "three free gifts to ease our way." Can you guess what they are? The gifts are nature, laughter, and music. Are there others you can add to the list? Good friends, faithful pets, a good night's sleep? Sometimes just quiet is a blessing. Think back to when you were a kid. What did you love to do? Did you ever just lie in a field, watch clouds, and chew on a piece of long grass? It gives you a real appreciation of the Creator.

How often do you give yourself permission to enjoy your day? Or even part of your day? When is the last time you laughed out loud with friends? I have to make a conscious effort for joy. Otherwise, the days slip through my fingers and another week, or month or year has slipped by. It's easy to bury yourself in duty and necessary work like a turtle, never looking up. Work and duty are good. But God put joy and laughter and beauty into this world, too. Live a joy-filled life. Notice all the good things God has placed here for you. He put a lot of thought into making an awesome place for us.

JOURNAL THOUGHTS

Read Psalm 23. Make a list of all the good things God has placed in your life. Enjoy them.

memory verses

83

Cast all your anxiety on him because he cares for you.

1 PETER 5:7

84

He who dwells in the shelter of the Most High will rest in the shadow of the Almighty. I will say of the LORD, "He is my refuge and my fortress, my God in whom I trust."

PSALM 91:1-2

The great soul that sits on the throne of the universe is not, never was, and never will be, in a hurry.

JOSIAH GILBERT HOLLAND

He who dwells in the shelter of the Most High will rest in the shadow of the Almighty.

PSALM 91:1

waiting for spring

There is a period when the earth lies fallow. The ground is not quite frozen, but not yet ready to bloom with new growth. Even the birds are quiet. It's a time for taking stock. Spending quiet time in the garden, sitting in the grass, on a bench, or slowly gliding back and forth on a swing, quietly praising and listening.

God gives us all the same twenty-four hours every day. We need to treasure time and plan out periods for personal renewal. Time for being instead of doing. For thinking, about God, about purpose, about things we don't understand in life. For dreaming dreams and writing down our vision from God for our purpose in life.

You may be at such a crazy period in your life that the very idea of time for yourself and God makes you laugh like a tired maniac. But that's when you really need it. You have to consciously carve out some time for a personal meeting with God. Schedule it in. You will be far more effective in doing God's will if you let Him renew your soul.

We all need times like that in our lives. It may be a time after something huge or hurtful in our lives, when we just need to catch our breath and lick our wounds and be comforted by God. It may be a time of life-changing discovery. We are being given a blessing. God is always waiting to meet with us, to speak with us, listen to us, and give us rest. Focus your attention on Him. Schedule a day with God. Enjoy some eternal time.

JOURNAL THOUGHTS

Is it hard for you to be quiet before God? Why? When is the last time you just sat with Him and listened and let your soul grow? Plan to spend time with Him every day.

memory verses

85

Be joyful always; pray continually; give thanks in all circumstances, for this is God's will for you in Christ Jesus.

1 THESSALONIANS 5:16-18

86

You are my God, and I will give you thanks; you are my God, and I will exalt you. Give thanks to the LORD, for he is good; his love endures forever.

PSALM 118:28-29

A branch's main job description is to remain connected. Its whole purpose is to receive life — and allow it to flow unhindered to its very tips. . . . Jesus promises that those who remain in him will bear much fruit.

LARRY LIBBY[1]

And we pray this in order that you may live a life worthy of the Lord and may please him in every way: bearing fruit in every good work, growing in the knowledge of God.

COLOSSIANS 1:10

fruit inspection

The first sign that summer is really here in Colorado is the start of the farmer's markets. Farmers come to appointed places, bringing fresh produce in their trucks, trailers, and wagons. Besides colorful vegetables, there are armfuls of homegrown flowers, new honey, roasted peppers, breads, and herbs. The best part comes at the end of the summer, when the fruit arrives. Paradise must be wonderful, because the taste of ripe Colorado peaches bursting with sweet juice is a small taste of heaven. The fruit is still good canned and opened late in the winter, bursting with sweet summer memories.

God promises to make us fruitful if we stay connected to Him. The sweet fruit of the Spirit is much more desirable than the fruit of summer markets. Spiritual fruits are to be used in relationships and interactions with other people. Take a prayerful look at your life. Regularly inspect it for good fruit. Is there ample evidence of it in your life? Is there a particular fruit missing?

Certain fruits grow more naturally on us than others. It may be because of the way you were brought up, your life experiences, or the nature of your personality. Ask God to grow good and perfect fruit in you so you can be a delight and a taste of heaven to the people around you. Stay connected to Christ, from whom you receive life. Enjoy Him, talk with Him, and listen to His counsel. Then watch. He is faithful and will make your life fruitful beyond your imagining.

JOURNAL THOUGHTS

What fruit grows easiest in your life? What new fruit do you want God to grow in your life?

memory verses

87

But the fruit of the Spirit is love, joy, peace, patience, kindness, goodness, faithfulness, gentleness and self-control.

GALATIANS 5:22-23

88

So then, just as you received Jesus Christ as Lord, continue to live in him, rooted and built up in him, strengthened in the faith as you were taught, and overflowing with thankfulness.

COLOSSIANS 2:6-7

part 8:

growing in
purpose

Let the herd graze where they may, but you be different.

TIM HANSEL, *HOLY SWEAT*

Where there is no vision, the people perish.

PROVERBS 29:18, KJV

beautifully unique

What if every garden looked the same? Two rows of yellow marigolds in the front, then purple petunias followed by yellow daisies and rhododendrons. That's it. No roses, no lilacs with their wonderful fragrance, no daffodils, lavender, geraniums, dianthus, lobelia. Beautiful but boring.

Some of my favorite gardens are found in unlikely places. Walking along one of the many beach paths in Oregon, kicking up sand, I come around a corner and find myself in the middle of a gloriously wild garden. There are long, feathery pink and rose flowers on tall, lacy stalks combined with brilliant blue and purple clusters on the ground that look like jewelry boxes brimming with gems. Placed on a background of beige sand and blue sky, the colors jump out.

There is a large private garden bordering a public path. The entrance has a small iron gate with iron ladybugs crawling on it. Every color and shape of flower possible is packed into this garden. Small fountains share space with the blooms; scattered throughout are whimsical stone and metal garden objects of art. It all looks very casual, as though the wind had scattered the seeds by chance. But, of course, it was planned purposefully, by a master gardener who knew each plant and how it would fit in the overall plan of the garden.

The best thing about gardens is that no two are alike. They reflect their creators' uniqueness. How about people? Did Jesus pick twelve identical men in identical suits and ties, all with identical minds? Did He only make friends with rabbis? Of course not. He hung out with men, women, and children who came from every walk of life. Tax collectors, homemakers, fishermen, businesswomen, carpenters, widows, shepherds, prostitutes, church leaders; everyone was welcomed into His circle. No one who desired to know Him was pushed away.

Jesus knew that everyone had a place in God's plan where they could fit perfectly and use their talents for good. How boring life would be if we were all alike. How would that reflect on the creativity of our God who made zebras and rainbows and fish that glow in the dark? Our Creator made thousands upon thousands of different types of plants and animals and . . . unique and beautiful people, like you and me.

JOURNAL THOUGHTS

Remember who made you. What is special about you? List at least five things and thank God for them.

memory verses

89

Each one should use whatever gift [she] has received to serve others, faithfully administering God's grace in its various forms.

1 PETER 4:10

90

So in Christ we who are many form one body, and each member belongs to all the others. We have different gifts, according to the grace given us.

ROMANS 12:5-6

Alas for those who never sing, but die with all their music in them.

OLIVER WENDELL HOLMES

Enlarge the place of your tent, stretch your tent curtains wide, do not hold back; lengthen your cords, strengthen your stakes.

ISAIAH 54:2

possibilities

When fall came late this year, and the first hard freeze hit my garden, I was ashamed to find some hidden failures. After my first zealous planting days in the cool spring, I slacked off. I had many beautiful plants in little plastic multi-packs. But life got busy and the weather became extremely warm. Not being a hot weather person, I stopped working in the garden except in the evening. Then there were too many mosquitoes. And a large, nasty-looking spider appeared in one part of the garden.

There were many reasons for not opening those packs and planting. I had them sitting on my porch for a while, but after they sat there day after day and didn't get planted (and sometimes not even watered), I put them out in the garden, among the already blooming flowers, planning to get to them soon. The small flowers looked nice there and got watered as the garden was watered. I planted a few in random moments but other things crowded my time. Then I forgot about them. In the fall, when the foliage died, I found them. They were still in their little packs, but they were dried up and useless. They had been paid for and delivered but never used, never able to bloom or fulfill any purpose. They never grew into their promise of beauty. What a waste.

God has given us every spiritual blessing, every gift. The trouble is, gifts have to be opened and used or they are useless. After a while, we may forget we even have them. Whether you are young or old, you have promise and possibilities. There are many things God wants to do in and through your life. He has given you everything you need to achieve them. Life is short. Don't hold back and become dried up. Drink some cool Living Water and let God put your potential to work. Your life can make a difference. Bloom in whatever ministry God gives you. The world desperately needs more love and beauty.

JOURNAL THOUGHTS

What is your purpose in this period of your life?

memory verses

91

Therefore, since we are surrounded by such a great cloud of witnesses, let us throw off everything that hinders and the sin that so easily entangles, and let us run with perseverance the race marked out for us.

HEBREWS 12:1

92

Learn to do right! Seek justice, encourage the oppressed. Defend the cause of the fatherless, plead the case of the widow.

ISAIAH 1:17

The Christian must not possess an inner motivation based on image, status, possessions, or accomplishments, but rather on being faithful to what God has asked [her] to do.

JEAN FLEMING, BETWEEN WALDEN AND THE WHIRLWIND

The harvest is plentiful but the workers are few. Ask the Lord of the harvest, therefore, to send out workers into his harvest field.

MATTHEW 9:37-38

getting dirty

My husband recently put in a beautiful flagstone patio and small garden behind our house on what had been just a dirt pile. Kids and dogs had dug up every living thing. Rain and snow turned it into a mud hole in the spring and anyone who went out the back door tracked in mud when they returned.

Before building the patio, my husband had a vision for it. He drew and tore up several different plans before he settled on the right one. Then we went to a rock yard and looked for the perfect rocks and railroad ties. He is a trained artist and has the eye of a perfectionist. It was very hot in the rock yard. I began enthusiastically pointing out many rocks for his approval. But he knew exactly what he was looking for and it took us a very long time to find it, as sweat dripped down my back.

Behind the beauty of every garden is a lot of dirty, sweaty hard work and discipline. Carrying heavy rocks for those pretty retaining walls. Bee stings, broken nails, and aching muscles. Planning within our budget.

Then digging, weeding, hauling, and lots of work on our knees. But now it is so enjoyable to sit there in the sun and delight in that fragrant garden.

Most things that are worthwhile and lasting are like working on that patio. They need plenty of prayer on your knees, patient planning, and hard, sweaty work. Is God asking you to take on a project that requires much resolve? A person in need, a child who is unlovable at the moment, something He has given you the specific skills to do, a person you can't stand who needs to hear about the love of Christ? Listen to Him. Whatever it is, pray, make a plan, and dig in. Put in the work and share in the bounty of the harvest. It will be so very beautiful when you and God are through.

JOURNAL THOUGHTS

For you, how does working for the Lord differ from working for people?

memory verses

93

Whatever you do, work at it with all your heart, as working for the Lord, not for men.

COLOSSIANS 3:23

94

Commit to the LORD whatever you do, and your plans will succeed.

PROVERBS 16:3

If we search for one word to describe the mission and ministry of Jesus Christ, reconciliation would not be a bad choice.

BRENNAN MANNING

Pray also for me, that whenever I open my mouth, words may be given me so that I will fearlessly make known the mystery of the gospel.

EPHESIANS 6:19

new life

Propagating new plants is lots of fun and you get new plants for free. There is quite an art to it. The method of propagation depends on the nature of the plant you wish to help grow. You can save seeds, graft parts of the plant, divide bulbs and tubers, plant cuttings in water, or cut and plant runners. There are certain basic principles to follow for good results and new plants. But it is God who gives new life.

Christ spent only three years in His ministry on earth. Yet there are millions of Christians all over the world today. Jesus trusted the people He taught to tell others the wonderful good news that God loves us. Those who knew Jesus then shared the gospel with everyone they met. They were never ashamed of knowing Christ.

Do you find it hard to share about Christ with others? It was never meant to be difficult. You have life-changing good news and you want to share it. Ask God to lead you to people who are searching for God. Introduce Christ to others as your friend. Tell the story of Christ in your life in words, and live it with love. Get to know your neighbors and people you work with in relationships that go deeper than the surface "Hi, how's it going?" Then the decision to trust Him is up to them. You are not to twist arms or pressure people. It is their eternity and their personal decision. And it is God who gives new life.

JOURNAL THOUGHTS

In your journal, list several people God brings to mind who do not know Christ as their Good Shepherd. Make a commitment to pray for them regularly.

memory verses

95

Everyone who calls on the name of the Lord will be saved.

ROMANS 10:13

96

"Not by might nor by power, but by my Spirit," says the LORD Almighty.

ZECHARIAH 4:6

We sing that song, "I Surrender All," but we're lying. Most of us have never surrendered all, because when you surrender all you don't worry about anything.

THELMA WELLS[1]

Pursue the things over which Christ presides. Don't shuffle along, eyes to the ground, absorbed with the things right in front of you. Look up, and be alert to what is going on around Christ — that's where the action is. See things from his perspective.

COLOSSIANS 3:1-2, MSG

rootbound

As a person who absolutely hates to move, I must confess that without the many moves and changes in my life, I would not have grown very much. Ever see a plant that is badly rootbound? There is almost no soil left in the pot to keep the thing alive. The roots are dry and shriveled because they can't hold water. Sometimes the actual pot holding the plant cracks open from the force of the unhappy roots, searching for room, soil, and water. The same is true for people, and this process is sometimes very painful.

We get set in our ways; we find comfort in our routine. But if we fight any change in our lives it may constrict us. It can cause us to stop growing in our faith and relationship with Christ. God is faithful, and will allow circumstances in our life that cause us to step out in faith again, so we can experience that He is faithful. Water that pools on the ground soon grows stagnant and unhealthy. The same is true with our "living water." It needs to keep flowing into our roots and then into the lives of others.

Are you rootbound? Has God recently cracked your pot to give you new opportunities to stretch and grow? God doesn't want you to stagnate. Stretch out of the pot into the hurting world. It needs you. And you need room to grow. Learn to trust the Sovereign Lord of all that was and is and is to come. Let God grow the roots of your soul into fresh new soil.

JOURNAL THOUGHTS

Look at the needs around you. Write down one new way to get involved. A very small thing on your part can mean a lot to others. Share Living Water with others. Christ has a ministry planned for each place and period of your life.

memory verses

97

The wise woman builds her house, but with her own hands the foolish one tears hers down.

PROVERBS 14:1

98

The LORD himself goes before you and will be with you; he will never leave you nor forsake you. Do not be afraid; do not be discouraged.

DEUTERONOMY 31:8

week 50

Love people and use things. Don't use people and love things.

ART DEMOSS

Give away your life; you'll find life given back, but not merely given back — given back with bonus and blessing. Giving, not getting, is the way. Generosity begets generosity.

LUKE 6:38, MSG

sundials

One thing I have always admired in a garden is a sundial. What an elegant way of counting time passing. Some days are absolutely perfect; we want them to last forever. Then there are days, weeks, even months that somehow get so busy and full that they fly by. Some days we just waste, as though we have an infinite number of them. Other days we desperately want to pass through quickly. Yet at the back of our minds comes a nagging thought that we are human and finite, and that someday we will beg God to put more days into our account.

Jesus had a comparatively short amount of time on earth, yet changed the world for eternity. Jesus spent His days and nights either alone with God or with people. He healed, taught, fed, and touched others. He laughed with them and ate and drank at their celebrations. He mourned with them and prayed with them. God and people were the focus of all His time.

We have to spend our time wisely. What does that mean? How does God want us to use the time He allotted to each of us? Take a long and honest look at your life. Write down a typical week and how you use your time. Then look at your gifts and your passions. Are you using the days wisely? Are you making the time count or letting it waste like sand running through your fingers?

If we don't spend quality time with God, we have nothing stored up to share with people. Sometimes the best use of our time is being alone with God, praying, reading His Word, listening, and enjoying His presence.

When I have my priorities straight (which is not as often as I should), I spend time with people. People I love and people who love me. People who need a caring touch on a certain day. People who talk, cry, and share their hearts. People who know me and love me anyway. People I've never met, like authors who took time to write books and share things about God that it would have taken me years to learn on my own. Difficult people who stretch me. Children who sing that Jesus loves them. People who are strangers to me. There are so many hurting, lonely people out there who need the love of Christ.

When you look at your watch, remind yourself to use your time on earth to live well for God. Live intentionally, with passion, awe, and delight. Make God and people your main focus. The sundial in the garden gives us all a finite number of days.

JOURNAL THOUGHTS

What does living intentionally mean to you? What do you consider a good use of your time? What does God consider a good use of your time?

memory verses

99

Teach us to number our days aright, that we may gain a heart of wisdom.

PSALM 90:12

100

Give, and it will be given to you. A good measure, pressed down, shaken together and running over, will be poured into your lap. For with the measure you use, it will be measured to you.

LUKE 6:38

Begin to weave and God will give you the thread.

GERMAN PROVERB

Commit to the LORD whatever you do, and your plans will succeed.

PROVERBS 16:3

plan to bloom

Can you imagine what a garden would look like if you just bought and planted things at random? Buy lots of brown bulbs not knowing their size or color, stick in bushes with no tags to tell you what type they are? No instructions on how deep to plant or if they need full sun or shade or what climate they can thrive in? What a mess it would be! Whether planning your garden or planning a year of your life, one of the main questions is "What do I want this to look like when I'm done?" What is your vision?

That's why New Year's always affects people so strongly. They either throw up their hands in despair, knowing they have failed at resolutions in the past, or they charge ahead with glee because it is a chance to start over, a time to reflect and plan for the coming year. They have a vision of their completed goal.

God wants us to live in today but have a vision for the future. As the Cheshire Cat once said to Alice, "If you don't know where you're going, it doesn't really matter which path you take."[2] But God shaped you for a purpose. He knows the desired outcome for your life and the best way to get there. If you insist on doing it without Him, it will be harder and take longer. And you may get lost along the way without His instructions. There are many things that God would choose for us that we would not choose for ourselves. I always wanted to learn life the easy way, and looking back, when God allowed that, it was my loss. Trust Him.

Dream big. Spend chunks of time just listening to God. Ask Him what your next step should be; ask for help in planning for the long haul. What do you want your life to look like when it's completed here? Plan to bloom and make life beautiful.

Journal Thoughts

Ask God for guidance, then write down one goal you would like to accomplish this month. Next, write one long-term goal, a big "what I want to do before I die" goal.

memory verses

101

"For I know the plans I have for you," declares the Lord, "plans to prosper you and not to harm you, plans to give you hope and a future."

JEREMIAH 29:11

102

Forgetting what is behind and straining toward what is ahead, I press on toward the goal to win the prize for which God has called me heavenward in Christ Jesus.

PHILIPPIANS 3:13-14

I came from God, and I'm going back to God, and I won't have any gaps of death in the middle of my life.

GEORGE MACDONALD, *MARY MARSTON*

There has never been the slightest doubt in my mind that the God who started this great work in you would keep at it and bring it to a flourishing finish on the very day Christ Jesus appears.

PHILIPPIANS 1:6, MSG

vista

A beautiful view seen through a long, narrow passage or a far-reaching idea stretching over time.

I remember the first time I ever toured a real mansion. It was called Stan Hewet (hewed of stone). I don't remember many details about the stone mansion itself, but I do remember the heartbreakingly beautiful vistas. As you slowly turned around inside the middle of the main hall, there were four long, visually stunning views outside in each of the four directions. Each view included a garden lovingly planned to give a unique serene vista. One view was framed with hundreds of tulips, daffodils, and every color of bulb. Another direction presented a flagstone walkway lined with an archway of huge green trees that met at their tips. There was soft sunlight at the open end. You wanted to rush out the massive oaken doors and fly down that sun-dappled path. Two other directions had equally glorious scenes.

Someone had planned ahead. They had been meticulous. They had stood on an empty plot of ground and looked into the future. They had seen the long-term implications of each brick, each tree, and each stone. They had taken the long view of things.

God doesn't always act in the time frame we may desire; but God is eternal. He is timeless. He created time for humans, so we could try to get our minds around the concept of forever. He sees the *really* long view. "This resurrection life you received from God is not a timid, grave-tending life. It's adventurously expectant, greeting God with a childlike 'What's next, Papa?'" (Romans 8:15, MSG).

The victory was won in the garden. Jesus begged God for a different way. When the answer was no, Jesus then consciously made a decision that made Him sweat blood. And with that decision, the meticulous plans were made. He looked into the long vista of eternity. He saw you and me there in the future. And He loved us.

JOURNAL THOUGHTS

God loves you and paid dearly for your life. It belongs to Him. Write down one wildly positive step you can take to avoid living a mediocre Christian life this year.

memory verses

103

Who shall separate us from the love of Christ? Shall trouble or hardship or persecution or famine or nakedness or danger or sword? . . . For I am convinced that neither death nor life, neither angels nor demons, neither the present nor the future, nor any powers, neither height nor depth, nor anything else in all creation, will be able to separate us from the love of God that is in Christ Jesus our Lord.

ROMANS 8:35,38-39

104

Being confident of this, that he who began a good work in you will carry it on to completion until the day of Christ Jesus.

PHILIPPIANS 1:6

how to spend a day in prayer

Adapted from the NavPress pamphlet by Lorne Sanny

"I never thought a day could make such a difference," a friend said to me. "My relationship to everyone seems improved."

"Why don't I do it more often?"

Comments like these come from those who set aside a personal day of prayer.

With so many activities — important ones — clamoring for our time, real prayer is considered more a luxury than a necessity. How much more so spending a *day* in prayer!

The Bible gives us three time-guides for personal prayer. There is the command to "pray without ceasing" — the spirit of prayer — keeping so in tune with God that we can lift our hearts in request or praise anytime through the day.

There is also the practice of a quiet time or morning watch — seen in the life of David (Psalm 5:3), of Daniel (6:10), and of the Lord Jesus (Mark 1:35). This daily time specified for meditation in the Word of God and prayer is indispensable to the growing, healthy Christian.

Then there are examples in the Scripture of extended time given to prayer alone. Jesus spent whole nights praying. Nehemiah prayed "certain days" upon hearing of the plight of Jerusalem. Three times Moses spent forty days and forty nights alone with God.

why a day of prayer?

1. *For extended fellowship with God.* Like most relationships, fellowship with God is nurtured by spending time together. God takes special note of times when His people reverence Him and *think upon His name* (Malachi 3:16).

2. *For a renewed perspective.* This is an opportunity to see the world from God's point of view. We need this perspective to sharpen our vision of the unseen and let the tangible things drop into proper place. Our spiritual defenses are strengthened.

3. *For catching up on intercession.* There are friends and relatives to bring before the Lord, in addition to our missionaries, pastors, neighbors, and leaders. Intercession is a well-known need, but rarely do we take the time we really need for this important discipline.

4. *For prayerful consideration of our own lives before the Lord.* This can be a time for personal inventory and evaluation. You will especially want to take a day of prayer when facing important decisions. You can evaluate where you are in relation to your goals and get direction from the Lord through His Word.

5. *For preparation.* If God gives us plans and purposes in our times alone with Him, we will be ready when either opportunity or tragedy strikes. We won't ever have to say, "I'm not prepared." Preparation is made when we get alone with God.

pray on the basis of God's Word

Your day alone with the Lord isn't a matter of sitting out on a rock and taking whatever thoughts come to your mind. It should be a day exposed to God's Word, and then His Word leads you into prayer. You will end the day worse than you started if all you do is engage in introspection, thinking of yourself and your own problems. God will reveal His thoughts to you by the Holy Spirit through His Word, the open Bible.

how to go about it

Set aside a day or part of a day, pack a lunch, and start out. Find a place where you can be alone without distractions. It could be a wooded area near your home, or your own backyard. An outdoor spot is excellent if you can find it — you can start by reading Psalm 104 and meditating on the power of God in creation.

Take along a Bible, a notebook and pencil, a hymnbook if you like, and perhaps a devotional book.

wait on the Lord

Divide the day into three parts: waiting on the Lord, prayer for others, and prayer for yourself.

As you *wait on the Lord*, don't hurry. You will miss the point if you look for some mystical or ecstatic experience. Just seek the Lord, waiting on *Him*. Isaiah 40:31 promises that those who wait upon the Lord will renew their strength.

Wait on Him first to *realize His presence*. Read through a passage like Psalm 139, grasping the truth of His presence with you. Ponder the impossibility of being anywhere in the universe where He is not.

Wait on Him also *for cleansing*. The last two verses of Psalm 139 lead you into this. Ask God to search your heart as these verses suggest. When we search our own hearts it can lead to imagination, morbid introspection, or anything the enemy may want to throw before us. But when the Holy Spirit searches, He will bring to your attention that which should be confessed and cleansed. Psalms 51 and 32 can help you.

If you realize you've sinned against someone, make note of it so you won't forget to set it right. Otherwise, the rest of the day will be hindered.

As you wait on God, ask for the power of concentration. Bring yourself back from daydreaming.

Next, wait on God *to worship Him*. Psalms 103, 111, and 145 are wonderful to follow as you praise the Lord for the greatness of His power. If you brought a hymnbook, you can sing to the Lord. This will lead you naturally into thanksgiving. Reflect on the wonderful things God has done for you and thank Him for your own salvation and spiritual blessings, family, friends, and opportunities.

prayer for others

Now is the time for the unhurried, more detailed prayer for others that you don't get to ordinarily. Here are three suggestions as to what to pray:

First, ask specific things for them. You may know some of their needs or prayer requests. Pray for spiritual strength, courage, physical health, and so on.

Second, look up some intercessory prayers in Scripture. Pray what Paul prayed for other people in the first chapter of Philippians and Colossians, and in the first and third chapters of Ephesians.

Third, ask for others what you would pray for yourself. Desire for them what the Lord has shown *you*.

prayer for yourself

The third part of your day will be prayer for yourself. If you are facing an important decision, you may want to put this prayer before prayer for others.

Let your prayer be ordered by Scripture and ask the Lord for understanding according to Psalm 119:18. Meditate upon verses of Scripture you have memorized or promises you have previously claimed from the Word.

"Lord, what do *You* think of my life?" is the attitude of this portion of your day of prayer. God may speak to you about rearranging your schedule or cutting out certain activities. You may be convicted about how you use your time. The Lord may impress you to do something special for someone. As you pray, record your thoughts.

Bring up any problems or decisions you are facing and seek the mind of God on them. Look into the Scriptures for guidance. You may be given direction from the passages with which you have already filled your mind during the day.

after prayer

You may reach some definite conclusions upon which you can base firm convictions. It should be your aim in a day of prayer to come away with some specific direction. However, do not be discouraged if this is not the case. It may not be God's time for a conclusive answer to your problem. And you may discover that your real need was to have a new revelation of God Himself. At the end of the day, summarize in your notebook some things God has spoken to you about.

two questions

The result of your day should be answers to the two questions Paul asked the Lord on the Damascus road (Acts 22:6-10). Paul's first question was, "Who are you, Lord?" The Lord replied, "I am Jesus." The second question Paul asked was, "What shall I do, Lord?" The Lord answered him specifically.

Don't think you must end the day with some new discovery or extraordinary experience. The test of such a day is not how exhilarated we are when the day is over but how it works into life tomorrow.

Days of prayer don't just happen. We have plenty of things to fill our time. so we have to *make* time for prayer. Plan ahead — monthly, quarterly, or yearly. God will bless you as you do this. Do it soon! You'll probably find yourself asking, "Why don't I do this more often?"

notes

growing in grace

1. Michael Yaconelli, *Dangerous Wonder* (Colorado Springs: NavPress, 1998, 2003), p. 103.

2. Dan Baty, "Love Supreme." *Discipleship Journal,* no. 137 (Sept./Oct. 2003), p. 24.

growing in faith

1. Jim Downing, in "How I Keep Growing." *Discipleship Journal,* no. 118, (July/August 2000), p. 42.

2. John Fischer, "Where the Pharisees Went Wrong." *Discipleship Journal,* no. 123 (2001).

growing in purity

1. Paula Love, *The Will Rogers Book* (Waco, Texas: Texian Press, 1971).

2. Jean Fleming, "The Practice of Pondering." *Discipleship Journal,* no. 123 (2001).

growing in wisdom

1. Ron Mehl, *Surprise Endings* (Sisters, Ore.: Multnomah, 1995), p. 120.

growing in joy

1. Larry Libby, "Maturity Beyond Measure." *Discipleship Journal,* no. 118 (June/July 2004), pp. 41-42.

growing in purpose

1. Thelma Wells, in "How I Keep Growing." *Discipleship Journal,* no. 118 (July/August 2000), p. 41.

2. Lewis Carroll, *Alice's Adventures in Wonderland and Through the Looking Glass* (New York: Signet Classics, reissue 2000).

about the author

SCHARLOTTE RICH is an editor, a teacher, and the author of several books, including *Grandma's Gospel*. Her latest book helps busy women tend to their spiritual growth through Scripture memory. Scharlotte and her family live in Colorado, where gardening is a challenge.

Journal

Journal

JOURNAL

JOURNAL

Journal

MORE LIFE-ENRICHING RESOURCES FOR WOMEN FROM NAVPRESS

Becoming a Woman of Excellence
This best-selling Bible study has helped over one million women understand who God designed them to be. Discover the freedom you have to serve and please God.

Cynthia Heald
0-89109-066-5

Becoming a Woman of Freedom
If you feel like your Christian life is weighing you down, this Bible study will give you a second wind and help you identify and lay aside the burdens that make you feel "stuck."

Cynthia Heald
0-89109-675-2

Becoming a Woman of Prayer
God designed women to seek Him in all they do. This Bible study will encourage you to become a woman whose life is characterized by constant conversation with God.

Cynthia Heald
0-89109-954-9

Becoming a Woman of Purpose
If your goals and success leave you feeling unsatisfied, use this study to gain a better understanding of God's purpose for your life—to love and serve Him.

Cynthia Heald
0-89109-790-2

To order copies, visit your local Christian bookstore,
call NavPress at 1-800-366-7788,
or log on to www.navpress.com.

To locate a Christian bookstore near you,
call 1-800-991-7747.

NAVPRESS®

BRINGING TRUTH TO LIFE
www.navpress.com

I am the way and the truth and the life. No one comes to the Father except through me.

John 14:6 NIV

But because of his great love for us, God, who is rich in mercy, made us alive with Christ even when we were dead in transgressions — it is by grace you have been saved.

Ephesians 2:4-5 NIV

Peace I leave with you; my peace I give you. I do not give to you as the world gives. Do not let your hearts be troubled and do not be afraid.

John 14:27 NIV

The LORD is my rock, my fortress and my deliverer. . . . He is my stronghold, my refuge and my savior.

2 Samuel 22:2-3 NIV

For God so loved the world that he gave his one and only Son, that whoever believes in him shall not perish but have eternal life. For God did not send his Son into the world to condemn the world, but to save the world through Him.

John 3:16-17 NIV

But God demonstrates his own love for us in this: While we were still sinners, Christ died for us.

Romans 5:8 NIV

The LORD is my shepherd, I shall not be in want. He makes me lie down in green pastures, he leads me beside quiet waters, he restores my soul. He guides me in paths of righteousness for his name's sake. Even though I walk through the valley of the shadow of death, I will fear no evil, for you are with me; your rod and your staff, they comfort me. You prepare a table before me in the presence of my enemies. You anoint my head with oil; my cup overflows. Surely goodness and love will follow me all the days of my life, and I will dwell in the house of the LORD forever.

Psalm 23, The Shepherd's Song NIV

[Christ said,] "I am the good shepherd. The good shepherd lays down his life for the sheep."

John 10:11 NIV

Jesus saith unto him, I am the way, the truth, and the life: no man cometh unto the Father, but by me.

John 14:6 KJV

But God, who is rich in mercy, for his great love wherewith he loved us, Even when we were dead in sins, hath quickened us together with Christ, (by grace ye are saved;).

Ephesians 2:4-5 KJV

Peace I leave with you, my peace I give unto you: not as the world giveth, give I unto you. Let not your heart be troubled, neither let it be afraid.

John 14:27 KJV

The LORD is my rock, and my fortress, and my deliverer . . . my high tower, and my refuge, my saviour.

2 Samuel 22:2-3 KJV

For God so loved the world, that he gave his only begotten Son, that whosoever believeth in him should not perish, but have everlasting life. For God sent not his Son into the world to condemn the world; but that the world through him might be saved.

John 3:16-17 KJV

But God commendeth his love toward us, in that, while we were yet sinners, Christ died for us.

Romans 5:8 KJV

The LORD is my shepherd; I shall not want. He maketh me to lie down in green pastures: he leadeth me beside the still waters. He restoreth my soul: he leadeth me in the paths of righteousness for his name's sake. Yea, though I walk through the valley of the shadow of death, I will fear no evil: for thou art with me; thy rod and thy staff they comfort me. Thou preparest a table before me in the presence of mine enemies: thou anointest my head with oil; my cup runneth over. Surely goodness and mercy shall follow me all the days of my life: and I will dwell in the house of the LORD for ever.

Psalm 23, The Shepherd's Song KJV

I am the good shepherd: the good shepherd giveth his life for the sheep.

John 10:11 KJV

Be still, and know that I am God; I
will be exalted among the nations, I
will be exalted in the earth.

Psalm 46:10 NIV

He calls his own sheep by name and leads
them out. . . . My sheep listen to my voice; I
know them, and they follow me. I give them
eternal life, and they shall never perish; no
one can snatch them out of my hand.

John 10:3,27-28 NIV

Ask and it will be given to you; seek and
you will find; knock and the door will be
opened to you. For everyone who asks
receives; he who seeks finds; and to him
who knocks, the door will be opened.

Matthew 7:7-8 NIV

And God is able to make all grace
abound to you, so that in all things at
all times, having all that you need,
you will abound in every good work.

2 Corinthians 9:8 NIV

And my God will meet all your needs
according to his glorious riches in
Christ Jesus.

Philippians 4:19 NIV

Do not fear, for I am with you; do
not be dismayed, for I am your God.
I will strengthen you and help you; I
will uphold you with my righteous
right hand.

Isaiah 41:10 NIV

Be strong in the Lord and in his
mighty power. Put on the full armor
of God so that you can take your
stand against the devil's schemes.

Ephesians 6:10-11 NIV

The one who is in you is greater than
the one who is in the world.

1 John 4:4 NIV

He calleth his own sheep by name, and
leadeth them out. . . . My sheep hear my
voice, and I know them, and they follow
me: And I give unto them eternal life; and
they shall never perish, neither shall any
man pluck them out of my hand.

John 10:3,27-28 KJV

Be still, and know that I am God: I
will be exalted among the heathen, I
will be exalted in the earth.

Psalm 46:10 KJV

And God is able to make all grace
abound toward you; that ye, always
having all sufficiency in all things,
may abound to every good work.

2 Corinthians 9:8 KJV

Ask, and it shall be given you; seek, and ye
shall find; knock, and it shall be opened
unto you: For every one that asketh
receiveth; and he that seeketh findeth; and
to him that knocketh it shall be opened.

Matthew 7:7-8 KJV

Fear thou not; for I am with thee: be
not dismayed; for I am thy God: I
will strengthen thee; yea, I will help
thee; yea, I will uphold thee with the
right hand of my righteousness.

Isaiah 41:10 KJV

But my God shall supply all your
need according to his riches in glory
by Christ Jesus.

Philippians 4:19 KJV

Greater is he that is in you, than he
that is in the world.

1 John 4:4 KJV

Be strong in the Lord, and in the
power of his might. Put on the whole
armour of God, that ye may be able
to stand against the wiles of the devil.

Ephesians 6:10-11 KJV

Know therefore that the LORD your God is God; he is the faithful God, keeping his covenant of love to a thousand generations of those who love him and keep his commands.

Deuteronomy 7:9 NIV

I praise you because I am fearfully and wonderfully made; your works are wonderful, I know that full well.

Psalm 139:14 NIV

And we know that in all things God works for the good of those who love him, who have been called according to his purpose.

Romans 8:28 NIV

I have learned the secret of being content in any and every situation. . . . I can do everything through him who gives me strength.

Philippians 4:12-13 NIV

Be very careful, then, how you live — not as unwise but as wise, making the most of every opportunity, because the days are evil. Therefore do not be foolish, but understand what the Lord's will is.

Ephesians 5:15-17 NIV

Do not be anxious about anything, but in everything, by prayer and petition, with thanksgiving, present your requests to God. And the peace of God, which transcends all understanding, will guard your hearts and your minds in Christ Jesus.

Philippians 4:6-7 NIV

Do nothing out of selfish ambition or vain conceit, but in humility consider others better than yourselves . . . look not only to your own interests, but also to the interests of others. Your attitude should be the same as that of Christ Jesus.

Philippians 2:3-5 NIV

For we are God's workmanship, created in Christ Jesus to do good works, which God prepared in advance for us to do.

Ephesians 2:10 NIV

I will praise thee; for I am fearfully and wonderfully made: marvellous are thy works; and that my soul knoweth right well.

Psalm 139:14 KJV

Know therefore that the LORD thy God, he is God, the faithful God, which keepeth covenant and mercy with them that love him and keep his commandments to a thousand generations.

Deuteronomy 7:9 KJV

I know both how to be abased, and I know how to abound. . . . I can do all things through Christ which. strengtheneth me.

Philippians 4:12-13 KJV

And we know that all things work together for good to them that love God, to them who are the called according to his purpose.

Romans 8:28 KJV

Be careful for nothing; but in every thing by prayer and supplication with thanksgiving let your requests be made known unto God. And the peace of God, which passeth all understanding, shall keep your hearts and minds through Christ Jesus.

Philippians 4:6-7 KJV

See then that ye walk circumspectly, not as fools, but as wise, redeeming the time, because the days are evil. Wherefore be ye not unwise, but understanding what the will of the Lord is.

Ephesians 5:15-17 KJV

For we are his workmanship, created in Christ Jesus unto good works, which God hath before ordained that we should walk in them.

Ephesians 2:10 KJV

Let nothing be done through strife or vainglory; but in lowliness of mind let each esteem other better than themselves. Look not every man on his own things, but every man also on the things of others. Let this mind be in you, which was also in Christ Jesus.

Philippians 2:3-5 KJV

God is our refuge and strength, an ever-present help in trouble. Therefore we will not fear, though the earth give way and the mountains fall into the heart of the sea. . . . The LORD Almighty is with us; the God of Jacob is our fortress.

Psalm 46:1-2,7 NIV

Consider it pure joy, my [sisters], whenever you face trials of many kinds, because you know that the testing of your faith develops perseverance. Perseverance must finish its work so that you may be mature and complete, not lacking anything.

James 1:2-4 NIV

Keep your lives free from the love of money and be content with what you have, because God has said, "Never will I leave you; never will I forsake you."

Hebrews 13:5 NIV

A generous [woman] will prosper; [she] who refreshes others will [herself] be refreshed.

Proverbs 11:25 NIV

Above all else, guard your heart, for it is the wellspring of life.

Proverbs 4:23 NIV

Whatever is true, whatever is noble, whatever is right, whatever is pure, whatever is lovely, whatever is admirable — if anything is excellent or praiseworthy — think about such things.

Philippians 4:8 NIV

Whatever happens, conduct yourselves in a manner worthy of the gospel of Christ.

Philippians 1:27 NIV

If we confess our sins, he is faithful and just and will forgive us our sins and purify us from all unrighteousness.

1 John 1:9 NIV

My brethren, count it all joy when ye fall into divers temptations; Knowing this, that the trying of your faith worketh patience. But let patience have her perfect work, that ye may be perfect and entire, wanting nothing.

James 1:2-4 KJV

God is our refuge and strength, a very present help in trouble. Therefore will not we fear, though the earth be removed, and though the mountains be carried into the midst of the sea . . . The LORD of hosts is with us; the God of Jacob is our refuge. Selah.

Psalm 46:1-2,7 KJV

The liberal soul shall be made fat: and [she] that watereth shall be watered also [herself].

Proverbs 11:25 KJV

Let your conversation be without covetousness; and be content with such things as ye have: for he hath said, I will never leave thee, nor forsake thee.

Hebrews 13:5 KJV

Finally, brethren, whatsoever things are true, whatsoever things are honest, whatsoever things are just, whatsoever things are pure, whatsoever things are lovely, whatsoever things are of good report; if there be any virtue, and if there be any praise, think on these things.

Philippians 4:8 KJV

Keep thy heart with all diligence; for out of it are the issues of life.

Proverbs 4:23 KJV

If we confess our sins, he is faithful and just to forgive us our sins, and to cleanse us from all unrighteousness.

1 John 1:9 KJV

Only let your conversation be as it becometh the gospel of Christ: that whether I come and see you, or else be absent, I may hear of your affairs, that ye stand fast in one spirit, with one mind striving together for the faith of the gospel.

Philippians 1:27 KJV

No temptation has seized you except what is common to man. And God is faithful; he will not let you be tempted beyond what you can bear. But when you are tempted, he will also provide a way out so that you can stand up under it.

1 Corinthians 10:13 NIV

Create in me a pure heart, O God, and renew a steadfast spirit within me.

Psalm 51:10 NIV

Repent, then, and turn to God, so that your sins may be wiped out, that times of refreshing may come from the Lord.

Acts 3:19 NIV

You are forgiving and good, O Lord, abounding in love to all who call to you.

Psalm 86:5 NIV

Though one may be overpowered, two can defend themselves. A cord of three strands is not quickly broken.

Ecclesiastes 4:12 NIV

Do not be misled: "Bad company corrupts good character."

1 Corinthians 15:33 NIV

Take captive every thought to make it obedient to Christ.

2 Corinthians 10:5 NIV

Set a guard over my mouth, O LORD; keep watch over the door of my lips. Let not my heart be drawn to what is evil.

Psalm 141:3-4 NIV

Create in me a clean heart, O God;
and renew a right spirit within me.

Psalm 51:10 KJV

There hath no temptation taken you but
such as is common to man: but God is
faithful, who will not suffer you to be
tempted above that ye are able; but will
with the temptation also make a way to
escape, that ye may be able to bear it.

1 Corinthians 10:13 KJV

For thou, Lord, art good, and ready
to forgive; and plenteous in mercy
unto all them that call upon thee.

Psalm 86:5 KJV

Repent ye therefore, and be convert-
ed, that your sins may be blotted out,
when the times of refreshing shall
come from the presence of the Lord.

Acts 3:19 KJV

Be not deceived: evil communica-
tions corrupt good manners.

1 Corinthians 15:33 KJV

And if one prevail against him, two
shall withstand him; and a threefold
cord is not quickly broken.

Ecclesiastes 4:12 KJV

Set a watch, O LORD, before my
mouth; keep the door of my lips.
Incline not my heart to any evil
thing.

Psalm 141:3-4 KJV

[Bring] into captivity every thought
to the obedience of Christ.

2 Corinthians 10:5 KJV

Fight the good fight.

1 Timothy 1:18 NIV

Submit yourselves, then, to God. Resist the devil, and he will flee from you.

James 4:7 NIV

Whoever claims to live in him must walk as Jesus did.

1 John 2:6 NIV

I have come that they may have life, and have it to the full.

John 10:10 NIV

Freely you have received, freely give.

Matthew 10:8 NIV

Watch out! Be on your guard against all kinds of greed; a [woman's] life does not consist in the abundance of [her] possessions.

Luke 12:15 NIV

And what does the LORD require of you? To act justly and to love mercy and to walk humbly with your God.

Micah 6:8 NIV

Be completely humble and gentle; be patient, bearing with one another in love.

Ephesians 4:2 NIV

Submit yourselves therefore to God.
Resist the devil, and he will flee from
you.

James 4:7 KJV

Thou by them mightest war a good
warfare.

1 Timothy 1:18 KJV

I am come that they might have life,
and that they might have it more
abundantly.

John 10:10 KJV

He that saith he abideth in him
ought himself also so to walk, even as
he walked.

1 John 2:6 KJV

Take heed, and beware of covetousness: for a man's life consisteth not in
the abundance of the things which he
possesseth.

Luke 12:15 KJV

Freely ye have received, freely give.

Matthew 10:8 KJV

With all lowliness and meekness,
with longsuffering, [forbear] one
another in love.

Ephesians 4:2 KJV

And what doth the LORD require of
thee, but to do justly, and to love
mercy, and to walk humbly with thy
God?

Micah 6:8 KJV

Above all, love each other deeply, because love covers over a multitude of sins.

1 Peter 4:8 NIV

A friend loves at all times, and a [sister] is born for adversity.

Proverbs 17:17 NIV

Whatever your hand finds to do, do it with all your might.

Ecclesiastes 9:10 NIV

Let us not become weary in doing good, for at the proper time we will reap a harvest if we do not give up. Therefore, as we have opportunity, let us do good to all people, especially to those who belong to the family of believers.

Galatians 6:9-10 NIV

Dear children, let us not love with words or tongue but with actions and in truth.

1 John 3:18 NIV

The entire law is summed up in a single command: "Love your neighbor as yourself."

Galatians 5:14 NIV

Pleasant words are a honeycomb, sweet to the soul and healing to the bones.

Proverbs 16:24 NIV

Though the fig tree does not bud and there are no grapes on the vines, though the olive crop fails and the fields produce no food, though there are no sheep in the pen and no cattle in the stalls, yet I will rejoice in the LORD, I will be joyful in God my Savior. The Sovereign LORD is my strength.

Habakkuk 3:17-19 NIV

A friend loveth at all times, and a
[sister] is born for adversity.

Proverbs 17:17 KJV

And above all things have fervent
charity among yourselves: for charity
shall cover the multitude of sins.

1 Peter 4:8 KJV

And let us not be weary in well doing, for
in due season we shall reap, if we faint
not. As we have therefore opportunity, let
us do good unto all men, especially unto
them who are of the household of faith.

Galatians 6:9-10 KJV

Whatsoever thy hand findeth to do,
do it with thy might.

Ecclesiastes 9:10 KJV

For all the law is fulfilled in one
word, even in this; Thou shalt love
thy neighbour as thyself.

Galatians 5:14 KJV

My little children, let us not love in
word, neither in tongue; but in deed
and in truth.

1 John 3:18 KJV

Although the fig tree shall not blossom, neither
shall fruit be in the vines; the labour of the olive
shall fail, and the fields shall yield no meat; the
flock shall be cut off from the fold, and there
shall be no herd in the stalls: Yet I will rejoice in
the LORD, I will joy in the God of my salvation.
The LORD God is my strength.

Habakkuk 3:17-19 KJV

Pleasant words are as an honeycomb,
sweet to the soul, and health to the
bones.

Proverbs 16:24 KJV

Be wise in the way you act toward outsiders; make the most of every opportunity. Let your conversation be always full of
grace, seasoned with salt, so that you may
know how to answer everyone.

Colossians 4:5-6 NIV

"Love the Lord your God with all your
heart and with all your soul and with all
your mind." This is the first and greatest
commandment. And the second is like it:
"Love your neighbor as yourself."

Matthew 22:37-39 NIV

We love because he first loved us.

1 John 4:19 NIV

For we are to God the aroma of Christ among
[the saved and the perishing]. To the one we
are the smell of death; to the other, the fragrance of life. . . . Not that we are competent in
ourselves to claim anything for ourselves, but
our competence comes from God.

2 Corinthians 2:15-16; 3:5 NIV

Call to me and I will answer you and
tell you great and unsearchable things
you do not know.

Jeremiah 33:3 NIV

If any of you lacks wisdom, [she]
should ask God, who gives generously
to all without finding fault, and it will
be given to [her].

James 1:5 NIV

Come to me, all you who are weary and
burdened, and I will give you rest. Take
my yoke upon you and learn from me, for
I am gentle and humble in heart, and you
will find rest for your souls. For my yoke
is easy and my burden is light.

Matthew 11:28-30 NIV

But those who hope in the LORD will
renew their strength. They will soar
on wings like eagles; they will run and
not grow weary, they will walk and
not be faint.

Isaiah 40:31 NIV

Thou shalt love the Lord thy God with all thy heart, and with all thy soul, and with all thy mind. This is the first and great commandment. And the second is like unto it, Thou shalt love thy neighbour as thyself.

Matthew 22:37-39 KJV

Walk in wisdom toward them that are without, redeeming the time. Let your speech be alway with grace, seasoned with salt, that ye may know how ye ought to answer every man.

Colossians 4:5-6 KJV

For we are unto God a sweet savour of Christ, in them that are saved, and in them that perish: To the one we are the savour of death unto death; and to the other the savour of life unto life. . . . Not that we are sufficient of ourselves to think any thing as of ourselves; but our sufficiency is of God.

2 Corinthians 2:15-16, 3:5 KJV

We love him, because he first loved us.

1 John 4:19 KJV

If any of you lack wisdom, let him ask of God, that giveth to all men liberally, and upbraideth not; and it shall be given him.

James 1:5 KJV

Call unto me, and I will answer thee, and shew thee great and mighty things, which thou knowest not.

Jeremiah 33:3 KJV

But they that wait upon the LORD shall renew their strength; they shall mount up with wings as eagles; they shall run, and not be weary; and they shall walk, and not faint.

Isaiah 40:31 KJV

Come unto me, all ye that labour and are heavy laden, and I will give you rest. Take my yoke upon you, and learn of me; for I am meek and lowly in heart: and ye shall find rest unto your souls. For my yoke is easy, and my burden is light.

Matthew 11:28-30 KJV

I pray that you, being rooted and established in love, may have power, together with all the saints, to grasp how wide and long and high and deep is the love of Christ.

Ephesians 3:17-18 NIV

Stand at the crossroads and look; ask for the ancient paths, ask where the good way is, and walk in it, and you will find rest for your souls.

Jeremiah 6:16 NIV

For God did not give us a spirit of timidity, but a spirit of power, of love and of self-discipline.

2 Timothy 1:7 NIV

Stand firm then, with the belt of truth buckled around your waist, with the breastplate of right-eousness in place, and with your feet fitted with the readiness that comes from the gospel of peace. In addition to all this, take up the shield of faith, with which you can extinguish all the flaming arrows of the evil one. Take the helmet of salvation and the sword of the Spirit, which is the word of God.

Ephesians 6:14-17 NIV

Am I now trying to win the approval of men, or of God? Or am I trying to please men? If I were still trying to please men, I would not be a servant of Christ.

Galatians 1:10 NIV

Charm is deceptive, and beauty is fleeting; but a woman who fears the LORD is to be praised.

Proverbs 31:30 NIV

If [a woman] is thirsty, let [her] come to me and drink. Whoever believes in me, as the Scripture has said, streams of living water will flow from within [her].

John 7:37-38 NIV

I am the Alpha and the Omega, the Beginning and the End. To [her] who is thirsty I will give to drink without cost from the spring of the water of life.

Revelation 21:6 NIV

Thus saith the LORD, Stand ye in the ways, and see, and ask for the old paths, where is the good way, and walk therein, and ye shall find rest for your souls.

Jeremiah 6:16 KJV

That ye, being rooted and grounded in love, may be able to comprehend with all saints what is the breadth, and length, and depth, and height.

Ephesians 3:17-18 KJV

Stand therefore, having your loins girt about with truth, and having on the breastplate of righteousness; and your feet shod with the preparation of the gospel of peace; above all, taking the shield of faith, wherewith ye shall be able to quench all the fiery darts of the wicked. And take the helmet of salvation, and the sword of the Spirit, which is the word of God.

Ephesians 6:14-17 KJV

For God hath not given us the spirit of fear; but of power, and of love, and of a sound mind.

2 Timothy 1:7 KJV

Favour is deceitful, and beauty is vain: but a woman that feareth the LORD, she shall be praised.

Proverbs 31:30 KJV

For do I now persuade men, or God? or do I seek to please men? for if I yet pleased men, I should not be the servant of Christ.

Galatians 1:10 KJV

I am Alpha and Omega, the beginning and the end. I will give unto him that is athirst of the fountain of the water of life freely.

Revelation 21:6 KJV

If any [woman] thirst, let [her] come unto me, and drink. [She] that believeth on me, as the scripture hath said, out of [her] belly shall flow rivers of living water.

John 7:37-38 KJV

You will keep in perfect peace [her] whose mind is steadfast, because [she] trusts in you.

Isaiah 26:3 NIV

But I will sing of your strength, in the morning I will sing of your love; for you are my fortress, my refuge in times of trouble.

Psalm 59:16 NIV

Cast all your anxiety on him because he cares for you.

1 Peter 5:7 NIV

He who dwells in the shelter of the Most High will rest in the shadow of the Almighty. I will say of the LORD, "He is my refuge and my fortress, my God, in whom I trust."

Psalm 91:1-2 NIV

Be joyful always; pray continually; give thanks in all circumstances, for this is God's will for you in Christ Jesus.

1 Thessalonians 5:16-18 NIV

You are my God, and I will give you thanks; you are my God, and I will exalt you. Give thanks to the LORD, for he is good; his love endures forever.

Psalm 118:28-29 NIV

But the fruit of the Spirit is love, joy, peace, patience, kindness, goodness, faithfulness, gentleness and self-control.

Galatians 5:22-23 NIV

So then, just as you received Jesus Christ as Lord, continue to live in him, rooted and built up in him, strengthened in the faith as you were taught, and overflowing with thankfulness.

Colossians 2:6-7 NIV

But I will sing of thy power; yea, I will sing aloud of thy mercy in the morning: for thou hast been my defence and refuge in the day of my trouble.

Psalm 59:16 KJV

Thou wilt keep [her] in perfect peace, whose mind is stayed on thee: because [she] trusteth in thee.

Isaiah 26:3 KJV

He that dwelleth in the secret place of the most High shall abide under the shadow of the Almighty. I will say of the LORD, He is my refuge and my fortress: my God; in him will I trust.

Psalm 91:1-2 KJV

Casting all your care upon him; for he careth for you.

1 Peter 5:7 KJV

Thou art my God, and I will praise thee: thou art my God, I will exalt thee. O give thanks unto the LORD; for he is good: for his mercy endureth for ever.

Psalm 118:28-29 KJV

Rejoice evermore. Pray without ceasing. In every thing give thanks: for this is the will of God in Christ Jesus concerning you.

1 Thessalonians 5:16-18 KJV

As ye have therefore received Christ Jesus the Lord, so walk ye in him: Rooted and built up in him, and stablished in the faith, as ye have been taught, abounding therein with thanksgiving.

Colossians 2:6-7 KJV

But the fruit of the Spirit is love, joy, peace, longsuffering, gentleness, goodness, faith, meekness, temperance.

Galatians 5:22-23 KJV

Each one should use whatever gift [she] has received to serve others, faithfully administering God's grace in its various forms.

1 Peter 4:10 NIV

So in Christ we who are many form one body, and each member belongs to all the others. We have different gifts, according to the grace given us.

Romans 12:5-6 NIV

Therefore, since we are surrounded by such a great cloud of witnesses, let us throw off everything that hinders and the sin that so easily entangles, and let us run with perseverance the race marked out for us.

Hebrews 12:1 NIV

Learn to do right! Seek justice, encourage the oppressed. Defend the cause of the fatherless, plead the case of the widow.

Isaiah 1:17 NIV

Whatever you do, work at it with all your heart, as working for the Lord, not for men.

Colossians 3:23 NIV

Commit to the LORD whatever you do, and your plans will succeed.

Proverbs 16:3 NIV

Everyone who calls on the name of the Lord will be saved.

Romans 10:13 NIV

"Not by might nor by power, but by my Spirit," says the LORD Almighty.

Zechariah 4:6 NIV

So we, being many, are one body in
Christ, and every one members one
of another. Having then gifts differ-
ing according to the grace that is
given to us.

Romans 12:5-6 KJV

As every [woman] hath received the
gift, even so minister the same one to
another, as good stewards of the
manifold grace of God.

1 Peter 4:10 KJV

Learn to do well; seek judgment,
relieve the oppressed, judge the
fatherless, plead for the widow.

Isaiah 1:17 KJV

Wherefore seeing we also are compassed
about with so great a cloud of witnesses, let
us lay aside every weight, and the sin which
doth so easily beset us, and let us run with
patience the race that is set before us.

Hebrews 12:1 KJV

Commit thy works unto the LORD,
and thy thoughts shall be established.

Proverbs 16:3 KJV

And whatsoever ye do, do it heartily,
as to the Lord, and not unto men.

Colossians 3:23 KJV

Not by might, nor by power, but by
my spirit, saith the LORD of hosts.

Zechariah 4:6 KJV

For whosoever shall call upon the
name of the Lord shall be saved.

Romans 10:13 KJV

The wise woman builds her house,
but with her own hands the foolish
one tears hers down.

Proverbs 14:1 NIV

The LORD himself goes before you
and will be with you; he will never
leave you nor forsake you. Do not be
afraid; do not be discouraged.

Deuteronomy 31:8 NIV

Teach us to number our days aright,
that we may gain a heart of wisdom.

Psalm 90:12 NIV

Give, and it will be given to you. A good
measure, pressed down, shaken together
and running over, will be poured into
your lap. For with the measure you use, it
will be measured to you.

Luke 6:38 NIV

"For I know the plans I have for
you," declares the LORD, "plans to
prosper you and not to harm you,
plans to give you hope and a future."

Jeremiah 29:11 NIV

Forgetting what is behind and straining toward what is ahead, I press on
toward the goal to win the prize for
which God has called me heavenward
in Christ Jesus.

Philippians 3:13-14 NIV

Who shall separate us from the love of Christ? Shall
trouble or hardship or persecution or famine or
nakedness or danger or sword? . . . For I am convinced that neither death nor life, neither angels
nor demons, neither the present nor the future, nor
any powers, neither height nor depth, nor anything
else in all creation, will be able to separate us from
the love of God that is in Christ Jesus our Lord.

Romans 8:35,38-39 NIV

Being confident of this, that he who
began a good work in you will carry it
on to completion until the day of
Christ Jesus.

Philippians 1:6 NIV

And the LORD, he it is that doth go
before thee; he will be with thee, he
will not fail thee, neither forsake
thee: fear not, neither be dismayed.

Deuteronomy 31:8 KJV

Every wise woman buildeth her
house: but the foolish plucketh it
down with her hands.

Proverbs 14:1 KJV

Give, and it shall be given unto you; good
measure, pressed down, and shaken together, and running over, shall men give into
your bosom. For with the same measure
that ye mete withal it shall be measured to
you again.

Luke 6:38 KJV

So teach us to number our days,
that we may apply our hearts unto
wisdom.

Psalm 90:12 KJV

Forgetting those things which are
behind, and reaching forth unto
those things which are before, I press
toward the mark for the prize of the
high calling of God in Christ Jesus.

Philippians 3:13-14 KJV

For I know the thoughts that I think
toward you, saith the LORD, thoughts
of peace, and not of evil, to give you
an expected end.

Jeremiah 29:11 KJV

Being confident of this very thing,
that he which hath begun a good
work in you will perform it until the
day of Jesus Christ.

Philippians 1:6 KJV

Who shall separate us from the love of Christ? shall
tribulation, or distress, or persecution, or famine, or
nakedness, or peril, or sword? . . . For I am persuad-
ed, that neither death, nor life, nor angels, nor prin-
cipalities, nor powers, nor things present, nor things
to come, nor height, nor depth, nor any other crea-
ture, shall be able to separate us from the love of
God, which is in Christ Jesus our Lord.

Romans 8:35,38-39 KJV